Talking
SNOOKER

Talking
SNOOKER

Fred Davis

Second edition

Adam & Charles Black · London

Second edition 1983
First published 1979 by
A & C Black (Publishers) Ltd
35 Bedford Row, London WC1R 4JH

ISBN 0-7136-2409-4

Davis, Fred, *1913–*
  Talking snooker. – 2nd ed.
  1. Davis, Fred, *1913–*   2. Snooker players
  Great Britain—Biography   3. Snooker
  I. Title
  794.7'3   GV900.S6

  ISBN 0-7136-2409-4

Photographs 1, 2, 3, 5, 7 and 9 reproduced by kind permission of
Snooker Scene. Cover and photographs 4, 6, 8, 10, 11, 12, 13, 14, 15,
16, 17, 18 and 19 by David Muscroft Photography.

Printed in Great Britain by
Hollen Street Press Ltd at Slough, Berkshire

Contents

Plates

Part 1
My Life in Snooker

1 The Old Days

Every so often in a sport something happens which puts it in an entirely different light, not so much to its own followers but to the general public. This was the case with snooker in 1978 when the World Professional Championship, sponsored by W D and H O Wills under their Embassy brand name, was seen not only by capacity crowds in the Crucible Theatre, Sheffield but, every day for two weeks, by a BBC television audience which grew from four million on the first day to seven million by the end of the tournament. To those who remember competitive snooker from its humble beginnings through to its first modest peak just before and just after the Second World War, followed by more than a decade in the doldrums from the mid 1950s, the colourful scene at Sheffield and the nationwide interest in the championship seemed almost incredible. Now, the event is coming to be accepted as one of the great sporting occasions and spectacles of the year.

My first recollection of the championship, though, is of being taken, in my early teens, to see my brother Joe, my senior by some twelve years, play Tom Dennis in the back room of Dennis's pub in Nottingham, a venue which was as far from a modern theatre as it is possible to get. In 1926, Joe had persuaded the Billiards Association and Control Council, who then governed both the professional and the amateur game, to sanction a professional snooker championship. As this sanction did not extend to any practical help or financial backing, the professionals, even the best of whom were struggling to make a living, had to rely on venues where overhead expenses were minimal and where sufficient paying spectators might produce some sort of financial return for the best part of a week's work.

When Joe won the first championship in 1927, he netted the princely sum of £6 10s 0d. The event rated only a couple of paragraphs in *The Billiard Player*, the magazine of the day, which reflected the general view that billiards was the real billiard table game while snooker was a passing amusement which was never likely to enjoy any great standing.

As my friend Clive Everton's excellent *The Story of Billiards and Snooker* makes clear, snooker originated in India in 1875 when Col Sir Neville Bowles Chamberlain was a young subaltern with the Devonshire Regiment in Jubbulpore. During the rainy season, the long afternoons in the officers' mess were spent on the billiards table where the parent game was less popular than round games like pyramids, life pool and black pool to which it was easier to add a modest gambling element. Pyramids was played with the cue-ball and fifteen reds initially placed in what is now snooker's familiar triangle; life pool was played with several colours, each player having an allotted colour for both cue-ball and object-ball and black pool was a development of life pool in that a player could attempt the black once he had potted his allotted ball. All three games flourished with the aid of a system of small monetary gains and forfeits. Chamberlain had the bright idea of merging the elements of these games into a new one which came to be called snooker.

Joe was the only person to see either snooker's commercial possibilities – though even this was largely in the immediate context of making a living – or, more important, the possibilities of the game itself. Snooker was regarded either as just a potting contest or, by those with a perverse turn of mind, as a game which gave them an opportunity to cause their opponents endless frustration with non-stop snookering and safety play, their potting being restricted to balls which were virtually over a pocket. Even today one sometimes comes across players who fall into one or other of these categories and I discuss the problems of playing them more fully later. But in general it is now taken for granted that some sort of balance is struck between attack and defence, between attempting nearly every pot and hardly any. In those early days, safety play tended to be negative, a far cry from the very sophisticated jockeying for openings that goes on now, and positional play was in its infancy.

Joe always had been a very good potter but when he started to utilise his billiards knowledge and skill to work out, on his own, the sort of breakbuilding sequences and techniques which have become part of every leading player's armoury, none of his contemporaries could extend him. As he was in the position of being an excellent player before anyone else had even realised how to play the game properly, that he would win those early championships was really a foregone conclusion.

Some of those early opponents achieved misleadingly respectable scores against him. It wasn't that Joe missed on purpose but, conscious of his superiority, he did not bother with safety play or perhaps lost interest and concentration once he was a few frames in front. It was in nobody's financial interest for the match to be decided early as the venue was booked for a certain number of sessions and the full number of frames had to be played out regardless. Dependent as the players therefore were on the gate, there were few out and out slaughters but at this stage of snooker's development Joe had so much in hand that he knew – and everybody else knew – that as soon as he started to apply himself fully there could be only one winner. I well recall, as I sat there as a lad watching him play Dennis, Joe coming over to me between shots and saying contemptuously, "You could beat this fellow, couldn't you?" Since Joe did not, at that time, entertain any great opinion of my game, this was not saying much.

When he returned the Second Class Billiards Trophy which he had won a few years previously so that the B A & C C could run a 'Junior Professional Championship', Joe was very reluctant even to let me enter. Because I was quiet, easy-going, without any obvious drive or ambition – certainly without Joe's dedication – he did not take me seriously and was afraid that I might besmirch the family name whose reputation he had built up. In fact, I won the event easily on each of the three occasions it was held.

Billiards, of course, was my first love. I played in the Boys (under sixteen) Championship when I was twelve and reached the semi-finals but this cut so little ice at home in Chesterfield that I wasn't entered for it again until I was fifteen. I went down to London, which in those days was a great adventure, so different from just dashing down the motorway as we do now, with two friends, Albert Barrett and Charlie Marshall. I won the championship but the prospect of public speaking was so unnerving that I put up Albert to make the winner's speech on my behalf!

Looking back, it seems strange that while, on the face of it, I was very quiet and in some respects lacking in confidence, I always had sublime confidence in my ability as a player. Indeed, although I kept this opinion to myself, I was firmly convinced that I would become world professional billiards champion. Professional billiards, of course, died in the mid 1930s when Joe, Walter Lindrum, Tom Newman and Clark McConachy so mastered nursery cannons and made the game look so easy that the average enthusiast hardly felt part of it anymore and stopped paying to see it. The amateur game still flourished, but professionals, myself among them, therefore had to concentrate on snooker so I never really played enough as a mature professional to acquire the consistency and depth of concentration which is the key to making thousand breaks at billiards.

The only time my self-confidence deserted me was when I realised that I could no longer see the balls properly. I was so self-conscious about this that rather than tell anybody I just played on, getting worse and worse, until I lost to Bill Withers, a Welshman whom I should easily have beaten, in the 1937 Professional Snooker Championship. We played at Thurston's, the holy of holies match hall which, in atmosphere, was like the centre court at Wimbledon and Westminster Abbey rolled into one. Our rating as a public attraction was such that our match was sandwiched between the afternoon and evening sessions at which leading players of the day were competing. It would have been an ordeal for any young player but not being able to see and having to endure Joe's fury afterwards made it all so much worse that I felt more depressed than I ever had before. Worst of all, in my own mind, I had virtually written off any future I might have had in the game.

I still didn't say anything, largely because I had it in my mind that I must not make excuses, but I did go to an optician who assured me that I would always be able to see perfectly with spectacles. He fitted me up with a pair of 'sportsman's glasses' as they were then called, which had swivel joints and could thus be uptilted so that I could look through them clearly, instead of in a distorted way, as I bent down to play. Having acquired these, my game improved rapidly. In the 1938 championship, I beat Herbert Holt and Alec Brown and gave Sidney Smith, then considered second only to Joe, a tough battle in the semi-final, before beating him in 1940. In fact, although he remained in the top four for a few more seasons after the war, he never beat me, level, again.

Sid's trouble was a fundamental sense of insecurity. An

13

excellent billiards player, he came under the wing of Willie Smith, world champion in 1920 and 1923, and probably the finest all-round player who ever lived. Sid, in the supporting role, toured with Willie week after week, a hard grind and not particularly profitable. When he did emerge from Willie's shadow and started to do a little better financially, he was obviously determined never to slip back – an understandable attitude but one which he carried to absurd lengths. He never rested, never relaxed and generally gave himself such a hard time that his game disintegrated. Basically, his game was sound but his clean, crisp cue action deteriorated to a very short stuttering one (not long after he had given me a real struggle in the 1947 championship.) His smooth swing back and forth degenerated into a curious up and down sort of motion and he disappeared from the competitive scene into the jungle of one-night stands in clubs.

Club exhibitions were and still are a very important part of every professional's income but they are very wearing. Sid made them more so. Not until the last couple of years of his career did he buy a car, though he partly compensated for this by an encyclopaedic knowledge of train times. Lumbered with his cue case, ball case and suitcase, he economised on taxis either by walking, using the bus or, on lucky days, being given a lift by the officials of the club where he was playing. Rather than book in at a hotel he would spend most of a winter's night in a station waiting room. When he was in London playing important matches afternoon and evening he would dash across town between sessions to earn a few shillings more by giving a lesson. He wrote for newspapers, he was the first television commentator, and with other bits and pieces he made a very good living but it so wore him out that his most precious asset, the form which kept him in the top flight, deserted him. It was a tragedy.

Among the other leading pre-war players whose careers continued after the war were Willie Smith,

Horace Lindrum and Walter Donaldson. Willie never really liked snooker and only played it under sufferance. He was a cagey, tactical sort of player and never became a fluent breakbuilder. In technique, I would rank Horace second only to Joe and possibly myself but he had, to say the least, a suspect temperament; Walter was very limited technically but potted extremely consistently and was a fierce competitor. Sydney Lee, now well known as BBC's 'Pot Black' referee, whom I had met in my first Boys Championship, had won the World Amateur Billiards Championship, then called the Empire Championship, but professional billiards faded out at just the wrong time for him. As his snooker was not in the same class, he was one of the profession's perennial strugglers until, by sheer hard work, he built up his coaching and exhibition commitments very successfully.

Herbert Holt, another player who fell short of top class, had been brought up in the billiards trade and concentrated on this and exhibitions in which he added a selection of tricks with finger spin to the usual range of trick shots. There were other professionals who played all and sundry for money, not always in reputable places. Stanley Newman, younger brother of Tom, was one; Alec Brown was another. Some kept billiard halls, like Jim Lees at Wellington, Shropshire. Whichever way you looked at it, though, it was a tough way to make a living. As the second or third best player in the country, I just about ticked over and even then only because I still lived at the family home in Chesterfield.

In the 1939 championship semi-final, I gave Joe a scare when he only beat me 17 – 14. In the 1940 final, Joe only beat me 37 – 35. (In the record books this became 37 – 36 as we played out the dead frames.) The cynics were not slow to suggest that Joe had 'taken it easy' with his younger brother but those on the inside of the game knew how wrong they were. Away from the table, Joe and I got along well and he was pleased that I had established

15

myself near the top of the profession. But at the table our rivalry was intense; having been in his shadow for so long it was my burning ambition to beat him, while Joe, who had informed me more than once that I never would, was determined to give me no assistance to do so. The 1940 final was the last time we met in the championship. I spent the war in the army and played hardly at all before, with only a few weeks practice, I went into the 1946 championship. Rusty as I was, I lost in the semi-final to Horace Lindrum, who then shared a record gate for the final lasting a fortnight, against Joe, at the Horticultural Hall, Westminster. Crowds of one thousand, two hundred per session for twenty four sessions created a very rosy vision of the future of professional snooker; ironically, less than ten years later, we were fighting for survival.

That 1946 final between Joe and Horace was typical of the many matches they played. Horace, with his good looks, attractive personality and attractive style, played some great snooker – when Joe let him. But as soon as Joe hardened his heart and let Horace know that he was playing for real it was no contest. Horace's trouble was his family background. He was the nephew of Walter Lindrum, the greatest billiards player who ever lived, and was thus saddled with the Lindrum name and reputation. There was a string of Lindrum billiard parlours in Australia and a strong Lindrum involvement in the billiard trade so it was not only on the playing side that the name of Lindrum dominated the Australian game. The family reputation was carefully cultivated, particularly by Horace's aggressive and domineering mother, so that Horace developed an undue sensitivity to losing which was exceeded only by his dislike of the strain of an out and out battle. Against an inferior player, or against an equal who chose not to bring it home to him that they were in a real match, Horace could play tremendously well but when he was put in situations where tension,

16

nerves and fear of failure came into it, it was a different story. John Pulman, who turned professional after winning the English Amateur Championship in 1946, told me with amazement that in his first major professional match, when he himself was understandably feeling a twinge or two of nervousness, that Horace said just before they started, "You can win, John. Let's just have a nice game."

Although he could not stand pressure, however, he was sensitive to anything which he saw as a slur on his reputation. When the *Sporting Record* sponsored a handicap tournament at Leicester Square Hall (the same hall as Thurston's but rebuilt after the war bombing and under new management) Joe ánd I were on scratch with Horace on the highest handicap of 23 points per frame. Horace took this as an insult and refused to play, though the better answer would have been to accept the start and walk off with the first prize. He quarrelled with Joe so when, in 1952, the professionals dissociated themselves from the Billiards Association it was not all that surprising that Horace refused to join us. While all the other professionals, except for Joe, who had retired from world championship play after the 1946 final, played in the world championship which the professionals organised, Horace chose to play the New Zealander Clark McConachy for the 'official' title. Everyone was well aware that this was a farce, for Horace, in a serious match, was now barely in the world's top half dozen while McConachy, though a very fine billiards player, was not in the top ten. Horace won by over half the game and returned to Australia as, to those who knew no better, world champion. Horace never played competitively again in Britain and only played on carefully selected occasions in Australia though he toured the world giving excellent value in exhibitions.

All this was very regrettable for, despite his limitations as a competitor, Horace was an attraction. It was also

17

unfortunate that Joe should have retired from world championship play after that 1946 final. It was always his ambition to retire undefeated and in the championship he never was beaten. But the fact that he maintained top form in exhibitions and other tournaments for almost another twenty years gave the championship itself an air of unreality. For the next ten years, whether Walter Donaldson or I won it, we always had to suffer the public's assumption that Joe would have won had he cared to enter.

No doubt Joe would have had his share of success – which no one would have begrudged him – but I did resent the public continuing to regard him automatically as no 1 without him earning it. I beat him on level terms three times under tournament conditions, the only player ever to do so, but this made no impact whatever. Whatever I did, I was just Joe's younger brother.

From the back mark, Joe won the *News of the World* tournament two or three times, which with eight or so players playing a round robin of three day handicap matches occupied most of the season at Leicester Square Hall. The professional game as a whole revolved round him but the championship itself degenerated into a two horse race between Donaldson and myself. Joe had always hoped that I would succeed him as champion but in the 1947 final Walter beat me quite convincingly. I was perhaps overconfident and certainly unprepared for the improvement he had made through locking himself away for hours and hours of solo practice. In that final, his long potting was as good (and in its consistency superior) to any I have seen before or since. His style was very similar to that of Eddie Charlton, who has dominated the Australian scene for about twenty years. Both have cue actions which are as straight as a gun barrel. The long straight pots and nearly straight pots go in like clockwork. Yet amazingly both Walter and Eddie tended to play almost as if they were always expecting to miss.

With their cuemanship they were capable of playing

18

any shot in the book but both were often reluctant to commit themselves to relatively easy pots if there was any risk of leaving a good position for their opponent. The safe pot often does seem more difficult if failure means a golden opportunity for your opponent but, at top level, the really positive players have enough confidence in their skill to pot the ball all right and simply concentrate on their next position. Walter's style was such that if he could go for a pot in a way which meant that he could hedge his bets by leaving the opponent safe if he missed, then he hardly ever did miss. By avoiding the use of side as if he could catch a horrible disease from using it, he inevitably sacrificed precision in his positional play in the interests of making absolutely sure of any pot he attempted. Time after time he would make 30, 40 or 50 with the cue-ball always slightly out of position purely through the excellence of his potting. At the first sign of danger, he would run the cue-ball away to the baulk cushion.

Only a player with Walter's amazing powers of concentration could play like that. In our first championship meeting, I grew a little impatient and, in attempting to create openings from half-chances, contributed to my own downfall. The way to beat him, unfortunately for the spectators, was to play him at his own game. In 1947, he took no chances and capitalised on my mistakes; in 1948, I took no chances and thus rarely presented him with positions which did not require a good opening shot to get in. It was not uncommon for a six frame session to last the best part of four hours but it would have been suicide for me to attempt to hit him off the table. I had to play in such a way as to oblige him to take some risks. Walter and I shared some big gates for the world final, which consisted of either a fortnight or week long match at Blackpool Tower Circus, but after we had contested eight consecutive finals, of which I had won six, he retired.

My opponent in the 1955 and 1956 finals was therefore John Pulman, who had been edging his way up the professional ladder for almost ten years. In his early days he had had some great battles with Albert Brown, whom he had beaten in the 1946 English Amateur final, but gradually came through ahead not only of Albert but John Barrie, (primarily a billiards player but at his best very useful at snooker) Alec Brown, Jack Rea, Kingsley Kennerley and the young Rex Williams. Albert was a very shrewd player and, notwithstanding a bridge which looked like a lump of dough, a pretty good potter and breakbuilder, although at top level he lacked just that shade of class or consistency which a champion has to have.

Alec Brown was an outstanding potter but not a polished breakbuilder. He won the *News of the World* tournament receiving 30 start from Joe and lesser amounts from everyone else but he was probably a better player before the war than after. Jack Rea, still much in demand for his entertaining club exhibitions and trick shot displays, was another tremendous potter, capable of winning sessions against anyone on his day. He once gave Pulman a fright in the world semi-final but I could never see him as champion.

Kennerley, who won the amateur snooker title twice and the amateur billiards four times before the war, never quite made it. In my experience, he was far too inclined to blame bad luck or good luck for the state of the game. These factors often come into a match, of course, but if you let them prey on your mind instead of accepting them philosophically you do yourself much more harm than good. Luck, in any case, only has a marginal influence, particularly in a match of reasonable length.

I first played Pulman in an exhibition at the hall his father kept in Exeter. Pulman senior was very keen that John should make the grade at snooker, so when he asked me what I thought of his son's chances in the professional game I was glad to be able to say in all honesty that his future looked bright. Joe helped him and a friend of Joe's, Bill Lampard, became his patron so that John was able to practise all day on Bill's table and live at Bill's house without having to worry too much about the fees which, being at that time an unestablished professional, were not always quick to come his way. Technically, John was and has remained very sound. He had a shrewd snooker brain, he was a great fighter and, at his peak, he was good under pressure. Fiery and temperamental in that his language was inclined to go over the edge if things were not going well, he is also one of the game's great wits. Some spectators, I know, found John more entertaining when things were going badly than well for it was then they were more likely to see some fireworks.

He has directed his wit at many targets. If a cushion has thrown a slightly unexpected angle then "The only thing these cushions are doing is stopping the balls falling on the floor." After a ball has run off a fraction he expresses complete bewilderment with "You need a map from the AA to play on this table." Of a slow opponent, he would say "If you played him a week's match it'd take a fortnight"; of a lucky opponent it would be "If he tossed up with a penny it'd come down half a crown." Of a player to whom he was not perhaps so superior as he liked to think he would say "The last time he beat me, a star appeared in the East." Invariably, if both he and his opponent had missed a series of comparatively easy shots, he would theatrically offer "Anybody care to make up a four?" He was never slow to express his displeasure at any distraction: a spectator moving, blowing his nose, whispering to a friend or – surely a case for the death penalty – eating a bag of crisps.

As a young player, he was inclined to be impetuous. Many was the time when, having been 40 or 50 in front with three or four reds left, he would chance a pot with the odds more in favour of fencing for a better opening, only to miss the pot and leave his opponent the opportunity to clear the table. On top of his natural impatience, then, would be the fury and frustration of having lost a frame he knew he should have won. Inevitably, over the years, experience gradually minimised these flaws although, in our matches, I always had the feeling that his impatience might rise to the surface in a crisis. When we met in the 1955 and 1956 world finals, I didn't have much in hand on either occasion and in 1956 I actually went into the penultimate session two frames behind before winning 38 – 35.

To remain steady and concentrate fully when one gets near the winning post is not, of course, as easy as it sounds. The tendency is to play normally, with good concentration and sound judgement of what to attempt and what to leave alone, until both concentration and judgement become distorted by thoughts of winning (or losing). One should not remain oblivious of one's feelings; there are times when I feel inexplicably confident on a shot which I might otherwise refuse. Sometimes, when a player has attempted a 'suicide' shot and brought it off without turning a hair you may hear him say afterwards, "I just fancied it." Equally, there may be times when you know in your heart that discretion is likely to be the better part of valour.

There are certain positions in which, regardless of feelings and doubts, there is no real alternative but to attempt a shot you feel you are quite likely to miss. In these cases, you should simply remember the basics – keep your head, don't move on the shot, don't snatch or jerk – and hope for the best. All this, though, is very different from attempting a shot that you know you should not attempt simply because success will give you the game or match. As soon as you stop treating shots on their intrinsic merits you are on dangerous ground. We have all done it (I know I have) but you should try to remain as disciplined, as clear-sighted and, if necessary, as patient as the situation truly demands.

22

The opposite but no less common sin is trying to make too sure by being over-cautious. If you have a useful lead, whether in a particular frame or on frames overall, there is sometimes a tendency to hope that your opponent will continue to make enough mistakes to virtually present you with the match. You tend to think that as long as you yourself don't make mistakes and give him the encouragement of some easy chances, then all will be well. The danger here, though, is that if you refuse reasonable chances you sink from a positive to a negative state of mind. If you do not adopt a positive and reasonably aggressive approach you actually appear less threatening to your opponent and you give him more breathing space to organise his resistance. If you simply wait for him to beat himself he may never do so. On the other hand, if you make him aware that he need only give you half a chance for you to wrap up the game he will feel under much more pressure, be more nervous of making a mistake, and so probably make all the more. It is as well to remember, however, that some players, having got into a losing position, feel they no longer have much to lose and by relaxing they start to play better. If, at the same time, you voluntarily concede the initiative, the combined effect often alters the course of the match.

One does not come to appreciate all the psychological factors of match play overnight. Many lessons can only be learned the hard way, but each one is an important part of a player's education. Like most promising players who eventually reach the top, Pulman gradually modified the tendencies which were costing him frames and became, by the highest standards, a very formidable competitor.

The two years we contested the final were the last staged at Blackpool. Television, which was later to be such a factor in increasing public interest in snooker, had quite the opposite effect in the mid 1950s when the novelty of having first class entertainment available in the home hit many sports dependent on attendances. In retrospect, it is also clear that the snooker public became bored with seeing the same few players contesting the semi-finals and finals, especially as the results were very predictable.

Elsewhere, clubs were having a thin time – again partly due to their failure to adjust to the challenge of television – and the club exhibition market on which professionals have always had to depend was contracting. At the best of times, one-night stands are a slog. Living in Llandudno, I spent most of my time in the north of England within easy reach of home but the travelling was still apt to get me down. In the days before motorways, smokeless zones and clean air legislation, roads were slower and fogs more frequent. In fact, I once recall being in a fog for a fortnight! Crawling along a bad road in thick fog, followed by an attempt to play, more often than not, on a club table which made it virtually impossible either to enjoy the game or display one's true form, was not my idea of heaven. For years I stuck it out until one night, when I went all the way to Pontefract only to find that there were barely a dozen spectators, I decided that enough was enough.

I felt that it was not worth my while to play in the 1957 championship which took place in Jersey with only four entrants and which, in the event, was won by Pulman. Instead of continuing to play by habit, I resolved to pick and choose my engagements. Indeed, when my friend Clive Everton, now editor of that invaluable magazine, *Snooker Scene*, asked me in 1959 how I saw the future of professional snooker, I replied confidently "It has no future."

2 Modern Snooker

After the 1957 event, no championship was organised for seven years. Occasionally, I played Joe on BBC television on a Saturday afternoon, usually in the worst of the winter when there was a risk that the outdoor sports on which the programme depended might be affected by the weather. In that pre-videotape era, the show was live and on those days when we fitted the snooker ration between two other items we were often told, in no uncertain terms, that we had only ten or twelve minutes to finish the game. In all honesty, the snooker was regarded basically as a stopgap material, though I suppose it did remind a few people that the game still just about existed.

Gradually, my interest and involvement dwindled and dwindled. One winter, I think, I never took my cue out of my case once. I was resigned never to playing seriously again until a phone call from Rex Williams in 1964 persuaded me to support his efforts to revive the professional game, his role in which has never perhaps been fully acknowledged, certainly not by all his brother professionals. Rex had been a professional since a few weeks after winning the Amateur Championship in 1951, having lost only a handful of frames. He was only seventeen and obviously an outstanding prospect. Joe tipped him as a future champion and perhaps he would have been if the professional game had not been falling apart at the age when he needed all the top class match play and experience he could get. There were, though, some question marks against his temperament; not so much against his fighting qualities and certainly not against his application, for he practised harder than anybody, but in his capacity to clinch winning positions and produce his best when it really mattered.

Technically, he was as good a player as Pulman, perhaps not such a good potter but maybe slightly more precise in his positional play and breakbuilding. But whereas Pulman became very good at identifying a crucial shot and getting it, Rex usually seemed to freeze and miss something quite easy when, on the face of it, it should have been plain sailing. Quite what was behind these inhibitions I don't know. Perhaps if he had managed a couple of really important wins these might have given him the confidence to go from strength to strength. We shall never know that either. But it is clear that the recession in the professional game could not have come at a worse time for him and that the problems which he had as a young professional were intensified not only by going so long without competitive play but by becoming so involved with business interests that, when the time came, his head was not as clear for matchplay as it could have been.

Nevertheless, in good times and bad, I have always found Rex excellent company and if anybody except he had rung that day I think my disillusion and pessimism would have outweighed anything that could have been said at the other end of the line. In essence, he wanted to re-form the professional association and to get the championship going again. If no one could be persuaded to stage a tournament then, he suggested, why not stage it on a challenge basis, as in boxing, with the champion accepting challenges?

Rex naturally wanted to play Pulman who had held the title for seven years without playing a match, but felt that I had the prior claim. I therefore played a three day match

26

with John at Burroughes and Watts, Soho Square and lost 19 – 16. I had deteriorated, not surprisingly; so had he, but not so much. John then beat Rex and then he beat me again 37 – 36 after I had led 36 – 35 and missed a great chance to win the next frame for the match. He then made four more successful title defences including one against me. Then, a chink of light appeared in the form of an offer of sponsorship for the championship, from John Player and Son, which allowed it to revert to a knock-out basis. This happily coincided with Gary Owen, John Spencer and Ray Reardon all turning professional within a matter of months, the first entrants to the professional ranks for seventeen years.

Gary, who did not do so well from professional snooker that he was able to give up his job as a Birmingham fireman for quite some time, had won the World Amateur title twice. Riley Burwat, one of the leading equipment firms, paid him, Spencer and Reardon a small retainer and used their names on a line of cues. Reardon, who was a policeman, turned professional on the basis of a tour of South Africa which had been promised when he had been there a couple of years previously as an amateur and Spencer, having fallen out with the amateur association on his return from the World Amateur Championship in 1966, when he finished second to Owen, turned professional on the basis of a small exhibition contract with Pontins Holiday Camps and the National Spastics Society. As these details show, there was no master plan to revive snooker. But these three newcomers gave the championship a new dimension and John Player's sponsorship, which had come about through Pulman playing a number of one-night stand tours as part of heavy promotion of their Player's No 6 brand, gave it another.

Snooker enthusiasts wondered how the established professionals would fare against the new challengers. They did not have to wait long for the answer. Spencer eliminated Pulman in the first round; Owen beat Jack Rea, and I only beat Reardon 25 – 24 by winning five of the last seven frames in a five hour final session. My own match was played at Stoke, a city which, for some reason, possibly connected with its place in the pottery industry, always seems to have a damp atmosphere. The table on which we were playing became so damp that if anybody used side the cue-ball flew all over the place. Ray was potting so well that he hardly seemed to notice the table's deficiencies but, in the end, in desperation, I abandoned all attempts to play my natural game and simply tied the game up, making absolutely sure of any pots I attempted but otherwise putting the cue-ball on the baulk cushion. It takes great concentration and determination to carry this policy through against a good player but, the way the match had gone, it represented my only chance. Ray, of course, was much less experienced than he is now and he was kind enough to say afterwards how much he had learnt from the match. We finished at 1.33 in the morning.

Despite this success, I was under no illusions as to how far below my former standard I was still playing. When you are playing night after night in public you acquire a consistency which you cannot reproduce just by playing occasionally. Nowadays, I am still selective about my engagements – at the age of seventy it would be madness to rush hither and thither playing every night – but I practise more than I used to. In that 1968–9 championship, though, I don't think I really appreciated just how much effort I would have to put in to make up those years in which I had hardly played at all.

In contrast, Reardon, Spencer and Owen had been playing in amateur tournaments – in which the general standard had improved dramatically – and were match tight and more than ready for those of us who had gone soft through lack of match play. It was against this background that I lost easily to Owen in the semi-final. Unfortunately for me, the match was played, as many were to be in the next few years, on a table of non-traditional design with a rectangular base instead of legs and abnormally wide cushion rails. These tables also tended not to run as truly as the traditional ones. I never played really well on a table of that type and, against Gary Owen, I was all at sea.

As comfortably as he won, though, Gary did not impress me. His potting, breakbuilding and safety were all quite good but his game lacked polish and somehow he never looked like a professional. Whereas someone like Joe could miss shots all night – not that he ever did – and still, through his presence, personality and the way he was dressed, exude professionalism, Gary still looked an amateur to me even when he was playing well. Perhaps this was because his personality never came across. Also, he had a surprising lack of confidence. At this point, he had always beaten Spencer (who had reached the final in the other half by beating Rex Williams but when I asked him how he thought the final would go his reaction was very negative. Consequently, it came as no surprise to me when Spencer beat him to become champion.

The following season, Reardon had his revenge over me in the first round and went on to win the title with wins over Spencer and Pulman (who had beaten Owen in the semi). Even at that early stage, Reardon gave me the feeling that he had great things in him. I rated Spencer highly also, but there was that indefinable something about Ray's temperament and approach which I thought made him stand out. Then, in May 1970, I suffered my first heart attack which, of course, put me out of the world championship held in Australia in November 1970. I recovered quite well, slimmed down from fourteen stone to eleven stone, but still underestimated the effect of this attack. This was not shown much in exhibition engagements but when I played Spencer in the championship quarter-final in Blackpool in October

29

1971, I found that I quickly became so tired that I couldn't concentrate properly – a hopeless state of affairs. This championship ended in February 1972 with an amazing win in the final for Alex Higgins (at his first time of entry) over Spencer.

The game was changing. In the decade or so that Donaldson and I were dominating the championship, the pockets tended to be very strict but they now tended to be, if not actually big, then cut in such a way as to help balls into pockets rather than keep them out. This inclined to favour potting at the expense of positional play and, on balance, aided the new generation of professionals rather than the old. The change from the Crystalate ball to the lighter and less predictable Super Crystalate, which was used for championship play for the first time in 1973, also had this effect.

The game was also reaching some new markets. The advent of colour television led to 'Pot Black' taking the air in 1969, thus giving snooker the most influential shop window it had ever known. Sections of the public, particularly women, who previously would not have known a snooker ball from a bar of soap, found snooker, with its civilised atmosphere, a refreshing change from the tantrums and violence one sees in other sports. Appearances on 'Pot Black' increased the demand for a player's services for club exhibition. In the case of Graham Miles, who won it as a substitute when I had to withdraw through illness, it was to change his life; from having a real struggle, he reached the relative security of being one of snooker's higher earners. Sports sponsorship was getting going in a big way around this time (another chance factor which was to benefit the game) and Higgins, not just through winning the 1972 championship but through getting into various scrapes and difficulties off the table, undoubtedly attracted a great deal of publicity.

One result of this was that the 1973 championship was staged on an entirely new basis at City Exhibition Halls,

Manchester with play on eight tables and the whole event compressed into a fortnight. Crowds were good, there was a lively, bustling atmosphere, the press took more interest and there was television for the last two days of the final. There were also some problems, particularly as regards concentration, for the crowds tended to move from match to match, often like a cavalry charge, at the end of a frame. You could start a frame with half a dozen spectators and before the end of it find that you had five or six hundred!

It was in this tournament, when I was playing Alex Higgins in the quarter-finals, that rain stopped play, which was a bit thick for a snooker event, even in Manchester. During a heavy storm, I was studying quite a tricky position when I felt a spot of rain . . . then another . . . and I realised what was happening. A rainproof cover was hastily placed over the table and Alex and I retired to the dressing room while the roof was mended.

This was a most interesting and at times exciting match to play in. It was the first time I had played Alex, who was and remains so unorthodox that I had to adjust some of the thinking habits of a lifetime. He is a gambler at heart and such a good potter with it that I could not afford to leave him risky pots which were likely to be costly if he missed them. He just ignored the percentages which were stacked against him and knocked them in. Consequently, I had to attempt certain pots that I would otherwise have thought twice or even three times about for fear that that was the only opportunity I was likely to have.

It was also during this match that it really sank in that I had to change my attitude to balls which were lying on cushions. In the old days, the pockets were so tight that to attempt a pot along a cushion save from close range and at dead weight – and sometimes even then – was suicidal. Accordingly, the leading players always tried in their positional play to cannon those cushioned balls into open positions. However, with the pockets now cut differently

31

for major tournaments, the new generation of professionals were showing how easy it was to drop the cue-ball behind a cushioned object-ball and run it down the cushion into the pocket as easily as you like. The funny thing was that, even when I started to do this myself, it didn't feel quite right. As a sort of hangover from my previous attitude, I never had the confidence that in fact I had every reason to feel. Consequently, I would rather not have to play this shot under pressure, just as my lifelong weaknesses, by professional standards, with the rest and on middle pocket shots seem to rise to the surface when tension is at its greatest.

Besides potting very well, Alex produced some extraordinary positional shots. He had the cue power to screw back enormous distances and attacked the game with such a flair and energy that no one ever knew quite what was coming next. He amazed me time after time with the new things he came up with and it is easy to understand why the crowds flocked in to see him wherever he played. One thing I couldn't get over was that, although the table we were playing on was running off quite badly, he could play from the baulk cushion to a red an inch or so off the top cushion and skim it finely to make a perfect safety return – just as if the table was perfect.

He beat me 16 – 14 after I had missed a great chance to level at 15 – 15. Needing pink and black to win (see diagram) I attempted the pink plain ball at medium pace so that the cue-ball would follow through and bounce off the top cushion for the black. After all my experience, I should have realised at once that this was not the correct way to play the shot. That table was untrue and, even playing at medium pace, I was giving the cue-ball a chance to run off before it reached the pink. Furthermore, in such a tense moment, the slower you play a shot the more likely your arm is to waver. The pink didn't even hit the jaws of the pocket. What I should have done was to thump the pink in, not with great force but nice and

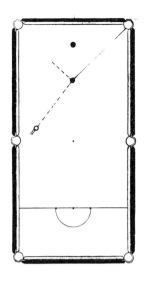

How I should have played it!

solidly, with a simple stun shot. I had done this thousands of times so heaven alone knows why I didn't on this occasion. It just goes to show that sound methods of play can never be ingrained too deeply.

In next year's championship, I had my revenge when, at Belle Vue, Manchester, I won the last three frames to beat Alex 15 – 14. I didn't play at all well for two-thirds of the match, largely because I had had my second coronary earlier in the winter and hadn't played at all for three months. Alex, who had won in 1972 and done quite well in 1973, was having problems too; though he was battling hard, he lost much of his confidence. He is a good competitor but away from the table his natural instability tends to lead him into all sorts of difficulties. On the other hand, he has a likeable side and, as an opponent, I have found him a model of sportsmanship and correctness. He has declared fouls on himself which the referee and everybody else has missed; he gets on with the game without complaint or prevarication, and on many occasions when he has lost in trying circumstances, he has swallowed his natural disappointment with as good a grace as anyone could be expected to muster.

Unfortunately, after beating him in 1974, my stamina ran out and Ray Reardon beat me 15 – 3 in the semi-final. I was in the driver's seat in countless frames but invariably did something stupid, and allowed Ray to reply with a useful break or even clear the table. I ended this match, incidentally, with the skin of the knuckles on my right hand looking as if they'd been rubbed up and down on gravel. The tables for this championship were installed not at the minimum height of 2'9½" but the maximum height of 2'10½". This may not sound much of a difference but the effect upon me, not being very tall, was that as my cue hand came through it caught the edge of the table on certain shots. When I mentioned this, I was assured – I tell no lie – that it was not the table which was high but the floor which was low!

In addition to the championship, there were a number of well staged sponsored events with prize money which, if not out of this world, was at any rate much better than we were used to. Norwich Union sponsored two tournaments at the Piccadilly Hotel, London in 1973 and 1974 and Benson and Hedges started their Masters Tournament at the West Centre Hotel. This was before it became a most popular annual event at the New London Theatre, just the sort of prestigious venue at which snooker should be presented, particularly in London. My record in these has not been all that shining. After spending most of my career playing matches of three days, a week or even a fortnight's duration, I have found it hard to summon up all my nervous energy and pour it into a seven frame match or, in the case of television tournaments like 'Pot Black,' only one frame. It is a weakness I have tried to work on, particularly in terms of altering my mental attitude, but I have found some of the difficulty a lifelong marathon runner might find if he was suddenly called up to race a hundred yards. The longer the match, the truer the test of ability it becomes, but the public's desire for shorter matches, like the cricket public's desire for one-day Gillette Cup matches as well as three-day county championship fixtures and five day Test matches, must be taken into consideration. There is room for various types of matches and tournaments but I hope I never see the day when the number of frames at present played in the world championship is reduced; that, I think, would be belittling our premier event.

Actually, one of my wins in a sponsored tournament, over John Spencer in Watney tournament at Leeds in 1975, convinced me that I could still compete at the topmost level. At this time, Spencer and Reardon were winning virtually everything between them so this success was a real shot in the arm. The 1975 world championship, though, turned out to be a farce from my point of view as I went all the way to Australia to play my match against Dennis Taylor in an ordinary club billiard room in which two or three hundred one-armed bandits were situated. As they were all constantly in use, the noise and distraction were incredible. It was, of course, the same for both of us, as it would have been if we had played on the floor, but it was all very unsatisfactory. In club exhibitions, one is prepared to do one's best on all sorts of tables and in all sorts of conditions but in championships players have every right to expect conditions as near perfect as anyone can make them.

The greater part of a professional's life, in fact, is spent not in playing championships or tournaments or television events but in slogging round the club exhibition circuit. For what is known in the game as a private show, the professional simply charges the club a certain fee but there are also sponsored shows where this fee is met by an outside concern like a brewery or tobacco company which uses the evening to promote its own products. The result is of no importance on these occasions as the idea is to present an evening's entertainment with quips, bits of by-play and, at the end of the evening, trick shots to provide a bit of variation.

On the road, I have inevitably had my share of mishaps and adventures. A lady who ran a club in Coventry once engaged me for the evening but made no mention in her letter that she was writing from her home address and not that of her club. When I eventually located her home, the only address I had, the whole road was in darkness. I was just about ready to give up. There was not a soul about except someone passing who directed me to a club at the end of the road. It wasn't the right one but someone gave me the correct directions. After an hour or so of hunting round Coventry I wasn't at my most cheery but suddenly we were there. "Lovely to see you," the lady beamed. "We were wondering what had happened to you."

For five years, Rex Williams and I toured on behalf of Watneys, whose representatives themselves arranged the programme. Occasionally, there were hitches. We arrived at one club to discover it had no table. "Where's the table?" we asked. "We thought you'd bring it with you." On one occasion, we stayed in the world's worst hotel. You couldn't stand up to get dressed as there wasn't room, you couldn't close the door unless you put your suitcase on the bed and the standard of warmth and comfort can be judged by the fact that the proprietor was muffled up and hooded in his duffle coat as he brought early morning tea. When we came out of the club after the show we weren't exactly bursting to get back to the hotel so when one of the club members came over to the car and said, "I know it's late but I don't know whether you'd like to . . ." Rex and I both shouted "yes" before he could even finish. We had a pleasant couple of hours with coffee and sandwiches before we had to face the night in the hotel. As Pulman would have said, "It was so bad that if you weren't in bed by midnight the bed bugs came looking for you."

Perhaps the outstanding incident happened on a day when the schedule somehow had us playing in Abergavenny one night and Norwich the next. We were on the last lap of the journey when, on a dual carriageway, another motorist decided to turn sharp right just as I was overtaking him. Taking evasive action, we plunged across the central reservation and down a grassy bank the other side, eventually coming to rest, sloping well forward, between two telegraph poles. What do you say in circumstances like that? I noticed amidst all the shaking that a piece of paper was half visible under the other front seat. "Is that a cheque, Rex?" I asked. When the case went to court we were completely exonerated and it doesn't take much imagination to realise that the accident could have ended very differently. Despite all, we arrived at the club smack on time. "Hello," someone said, "We were wondering where you'd got to."

In the 1976 world championship at Wythenshawe Forum I lost 15–13 in the quarter-final to Eddie Charlton. I had, at last, regained my stamina after my two coronaries and I was in the mood to play well but it turned out to be one of those close matches which, for no particular reason, just happened to go the other way. Eddie has such a ramrod straight cue action that he is very consistent, but his failure to win the championship comes down largely to his reluctance to extend his range of shots by using side and generally being more enterprising. If his opponent makes mistakes, Eddie will bury him but if a top class opponent is at the top of his form, Eddie will always finish on the losing side. You need more daring and flair than appears to be in his make-up to alter the course of events.

Despite losing this particular match, my own form remained good and the week after the championship I reached the final of the professional tournament at Pontins. I lost 11–10 to Reardon and, if I had potted a brown in the last frame, I would have won. This has remained my best performance at Pontins, whose May Festival of snooker at Prestatyn has become one of the game's most popular institutions since it started in 1974. Win or lose, this is invariably a very enjoyable, if hectic, week.

Apart from the professional tournament, the professionals all play in the Open, in which the eight hundred odd amateurs who start the week are whittled down to twenty-four by the time the professionals join them in the last 32. The amateurs all receive 25 or, in 1978, 30 per frame, so they obviously have every chance to do some giant-killing. There is a very competitive but very friendly atmosphere; everyone wants to talk snooker; and if the autograph hunters do become a little wearing by the end of the week this is a small price to pay for an event which stimulates so much interest in the game.

My preparations for the 1977 championship which was held for the first time at the Crucible Theatre, Sheffield, went well. I was confident and striking the ball well. When it came to the day of my first round match with John Pulman, though, I was unaccountably out of touch. John, in contrast, played better than I had seen for about five years, for he had forsaken what had become his casual approach to competition by practising hard and cutting down on some of the good things of life.

Trailing 6 – 11 going into the final session, I made John sweat by recovering to 12 – 12 but he won the decider and not only put me out in the first round but, because of the points system the World Professional Billiards and Snooker Association uses to determine its rankings, into the qualifying competition for the 1978 championship.

The system is that the top eight are allowed into the competition proper of sixteen players as of right but that everyone ranked below no 8 has to slog through the qualifying competition. This was played at Romiley Forum, Stockport where I was drawn against John Virgo, a very capable professional from Manchester, typical of the group of hungry young players who were trying to take advantage of some of the excellent opportunities which now exist in the game. My previous competitive outings of the season had consisted of a 5—0 defeat by Patsy Fagan in the new Super Crystalate United Kingdom Championship at Blackpool and a 4—3 defeat by Graham Miles (after leading 3—1) in the Benson and Hedges Masters so, although I felt I was hitting the ball quite well, I was lacking the confidence which comes through winning. After trailing 3—7, I won 9—8. I felt as if I had won the championship, instead of having merely earned the right to take part in it.

Having scraped through the qualifying competition so narrowly, I was more relaxed in Sheffield, beating Dennis Taylor and Patsy Fagan before losing 18−16 in the semifinal to Perrie Mans, the South African champion. I held a high opinion of Fagan, who has a very solid game and a good temperament. When a position is not straight-forward, he tends to take a long time to work things out and this may well, in the long run, put him off more than it puts off his opponents but, once I had beaten him, I fancied my chance to reach the final.

Although Mans had beaten Spencer, I thought right until the last frame that I should win. There was a day's rest between my quarter-final and the semi but instead of this rest doing me good, it allowed me to let myself down mentally and gave me the problem of recapturing the desired mood for the semi-final. I started reasonably well and led 5 − 2 but things went badly wrong in the second session when Perrie overtook me to lead 8 − 6. Carelessly, I had not considered the implications of playing an afternoon followed by an evening session rather than a morning and evening session, which had been my routine so far. The afternoon session dragged on a bit and I suddenly found myself with time only to rush back to my hotel, change into evening dress and get back again to the theatre just in time to play. What I should have been doing, of course, was putting my feet up in the dressing room and leisurely recharging my batteries. Instead, all the rushing about left me tense and tired even before I started the evening session.

I found Perrie an awkward opponent. He is an exceptionally good single ball potter and if there was a ball on, even at long distance, he invariably knocked it in. His positional play is comparatively weak – which is perhaps just as well for the rest of us – but the tactical side of his game was much better than I had expected from simply observing him as a spectator. In his matches, too, the colours seem to spend more time away from their respective spots than is usual in top class snooker and many of these frames tend to develop in a way which suits his style. When the yellow, green and brown are disturbed from their spots it often means that the cue-ball has no colour to 'hide' behind, when a player attempts a safety shot from a red in the top half of the table. As Perrie is such a good long potter, there were many situations in which I felt that it was impossible to leave the cue-ball safe.

After three sessions he led 13 – 8 and after four 16 – 12 but in the final session I came back to 14 – 16 only to miss a straight pink off its spot which would have given me 15 – 16! How I missed that pink I shall never know. I didn't rush. It seemed, from looking at the videotape afterwards, that I did everything right. But the pink didn't go in the pocket. Even then I thought I had a chance as I won the next two frames, but Perrie got in with his best break of the match, 60, in the 34th frame and clinched it 18 – 16. Naturally, I was disappointed to lose, especially as I felt that I had plenty of strength left for the final against Reardon. On the other hand, I was pleased to have done well and the reception I received from the crowd whenever I played was very pleasing.

It was very sad that Joe should be taken ill when he was

watching the match and, though he recovered from the immediate operation, he died a few months later. It may have been unwise at his age – he was seventy-seven – to come up from London, do a couple of television interviews and watch a tense match in which he had a family interest but I am glad that he was able to see the marvellous scene at the Crucible Theatre and reflect on how far the game in which he had played such a vital role had progressed. Joe, in any case, was not the sort of man to spend his old age in a pair of carpet slippers sinking deeper and deeper into an armchair; he liked to be up and about, doing and seeing things.

The 1979 World Championship, fulfilled all the hopes raised by the 1978 event. This time, the excitement centred round a new champion, Terry Griffiths, a young Welshman who had turned professional only a few months previously.

For someone like Terry, with no experience of a series of long matches, to win the title was truly incredible, probably the most remarkable achievement the game has ever known. The only possible comparison is Higgins winning at his first attempt in 1972, but the game was nothing like as big then and the championship was broken up over the whole season, not concentrated into a fortnight as it is now. Terry was involved in two especially memorable matches, a 13–12 quarter-final win over Higgins and a 19–17 semi-final win over Charlton which was a triumph of will power and mental stamina.

I was disappointed at my own performance in going out 13–4 to Charlton in the quarter-finals. I tried to attack early on, believing this to be the best policy, but missed too many shots I should have got. I was soon 0–5 down and never looked like recovering. Earlier, I had beaten Kirk Stevens, a 20-year-old Canadian, 13–8. Kirk potted extremely well but when I slowed the game down his inexperience became apparent. I was sure, though, that Kirk and many other fine young players were soon going to make big names for themselves. For Terry to win the championship out of the blue certainly gave them new inspiration.

I beat Kirk again 5–4 in the 1981 Benson and Hedges Masters, when these shortcomings were still apparent, but with regular exposure to top class competition he has clearly improved, developing some craft in his safety play and not being so inclined to try to hit his way out of trouble with a desperate attempt at some unlikely pot – even though he is still not above resorting to this on occasion.

It has been good to see Canada emerging as such a strong force in the game in the last few years. Bill Werbeniuk, though he does not fit the usual mould of Snooker players, has become a player to be reckoned with and Cliff Thorburn not only reached the world final in 1977, when he lost to Spencer, but in 1980 went one better when he beat Higgins in the final.

This was a fine achievement, all the more so since Cliff is not blessed with outstanding natural ability. Higgins did let him off the hook when he led 9–5 only to throw all caution to the winds in losing the last four frames of the first day's play. Thorburn just scraped home 18–16 but the title quickly became almost a burden to him.

So much is expected of a champion everywhere he plays that he is quick to sense when he is disappointing the public. In Cliff's case it was virtually impossible for him to satisfy them, especially in exhibition engagements, because his best qualities – precise cue-ball control, concentration and tenacity – do not set the blood racing.

He is slow, methodical and cannot play to anything like his best standard in the comparatively effortless way that certain other players do. He is essentially a match player – and a very good one – who can earn heavily in the context of modern Snooker because there are so many tournaments to play in that he does not have to bother all that much with exhibitions. In the days when the scene was largely exhibitions with only a couple of tournaments thrown in, Cliff would have found it hard going, not because he wasn't a good player but because he is the wrong sort of good player.

One way or another, the pressure of being champion cracked him for a while and he could not settle to living permanently in England. Two seasons after he won the title, he did not win a match from October to the end of the season in May.

Sensibly, he decided to return to Canada, living among his friends, and fly over to England for tournaments. It has already become the pattern for players to concentrate more on preparing and practising for tournaments rather than exhausting themselves rushing from one exhibition to another, and it may even become common for players to pick and choose their tournaments on the grounds that they can only produce peak performance and make maximum mental effort a few times a year.

This, of course, would have been inconceivable even ten years ago. Whenever a tournament was organised, everyone wanted to play in it because they were never sure that there would ever be another!

After his disasters of 1981–2, Cliff looked more his old self in 1982–3, winning the Benson and Hedges Masters and then skipping a couple of tournaments before coming back to reach the final of the world championship. Unfortunately, the strain of beating Terry Griffiths 13–12, Kirk Stevens 13–12 and Tony Knowles 16–15 drained him so much that he had nothing left and Steve Davis beat him with a session to spare in the final.

Earlier in the season, Thorburn, Stevens and Werbeniuk had won the State Express World Team Classic for Canada after Wales had won it in 1979 and 1980, and England in 1981. For the 1979 event, because my ranking justified it, I was the England captain.

This is a tournament which television has made possible and the public, both at the venue and in front of their television sets, seem to like it. For most of my career there have been all too few promoters who thought a profit could be made if they had to pay two players to play each other, never mind two teams of three, but as more income comes into the game through television and sponsorship promoters are not so dependent on gate money.

From a playing point of view, this tournament is not my cup of tea because matches of the best of three frames are such a lottery. To a lifelong slow starter like me they seem to end before I have begun to play properly. This is also true of another new televised tournament, the Yamaha International Masters, which started in 1981. This consists of a series of four man leagues each playing matches of the best of three frames. Again, the public seem to like it as it gives them the opportunity to see a lot of players in action at the same session.

Another new idea was the Hofmeister World Doubles, which started in 1982. Actually, back in the fifties, Joe, John Pulman, Walter Donaldson and myself had played a couple of weeks matches in which Joe's partnership was sponsored by the News of the World and mine by the Evening News. We packed out Leicester Square Hall but the experiment was not repeated; the problem of paying four players rather than two again rearing its ugly head. A world doubles championship was never even contemplated in those days because not enough partnerships could have been assembled to make it credible.

I must say, though, that of all the variants of single combat, straight matchplay which it seems necessary to offer the public, I prefer doubles. Having four

44

players involved in a frame rather than two prevents anyone working up much fluency but there is scope for tactics and an unselfish team effort can often prevail over a partnership which, as individuals, seems much superior.

I well remember, when Walter Donaldson and I were playing Joe and John Pulman at Leicester Square that we decided that whoever played in front of Joe, who was obviously the danger man, would concentrate on leaving him with the cue-ball safe on the baulk cushion. In one session, Joe did not, I believe, play a single shot in the black spot area. Hating as he did to be kept out of the limelight, he fumed and fretted and John did almost all his team's scoring in that session. When someone afterwards congratulated John on holding the side together, Joe piped up in all seriousness: "Don't forget, I played some pretty good safety."

How Joe would have loved today's scene! Prestigious venues, big crowds, hours of television coverage, acres of space in the newspapers. He would have thrived on it. Obviously, with more tournaments and much shorter matches, he would have lost a few but not, I believe, very many. He was always a very quick starter, so important in the best of nine frames matches of which even some quite important tournaments now consist, and the force of his personality brought the best out of him – and sometimes the worst out of his opponents – in competition.

Having believed for years that all film recordings of Joe in action had been lost, I was delighted to see the BBC unearth one of him making a century break in one of the Grandstand programmes of the fifties. People have told me how surprised they were to note how fast he was – every bit as fast as Higgins ever was.

The only player of today whom I could ever begin to compare with Joe is Steve Davis, though real greatness in my book has to be assessed over a long period. When I saw Steve win the Pontins Open in 1978, I realised from the straightness of his cue delivery that he was likely to be exceptional. He turned professional later that year and when Doug Mountjoy won the Coral United Kingdom championship, Coral's offered him a fifteen venue British tour with 'their' champion. Surprisingly, Mountjoy turned the tour down and I accepted the invitation to take his place. By the middle of the tour I felt sure that Steve was a future world champion.

Steve duly won the Coral UK the following season and for about eighteen months, a period which included the 1981 world title, most other tournaments as well. He came unstuck by trying to cram too much into his schedule and lost to Tony Knowles in the first round of the 1982 world championship. Terry Griffiths, who had seemed his only really serious rival for the title, immediately lost as well and Alex, whom everyone had just about written off in terms of winning the championship again, rose to the opportunity which was offered and won it.

Considering his lifestyle and personality, Alex has lasted remarkably well. Apart from Steve, he can still beat anyone on his day but he doesn't have so many days as he used to. Steve has so often beaten him by big margins that it would surprise me if Alex ever beat him in anything important. But with Steve gone, Alex found inspiration in some desperate finishes and won his second championship ten years after his first. The following season, though, the extra pressure of being champion was again evident and he didn't do all that well, though he lost only 16–15 in the final of the Coral UK, to Terry after Terry had beaten Steve.

Terry, in my opinion, is number two to Steve at the moment. He has had a few disappointments in the world championship but he has won the Benson and

Hedges Masters, the Benson and Hedges Irish Masters three times and a couple of other tournaments besides.

Since he won the championship he has grown slower and more cautious – I think Steve has too – as players tend to when they have some status to defend. He has a lovely action and I cannot understand why he has tinkered about with it in the last season or so. Steve crushed him psychologically for a while but, greatly to his credit, Terry has battled back to beat him a few times and has a better record against Steve than any other player has been able to muster.

Looking round the other players, it is a little sad that John Spencer is only a shadow of the player that he was. He won the world title in 1969 and 1970 and in the early seventies most of the other tournaments as well but it was only for a few years that he was really a great player.

In some strange way he lost his easy, natural cue action and his confidence with it, although he did win the world title again in 1977. Perhaps he is just a little too easy-going to work on his game with quite the determination other players have shown; perhaps a change in financial circumstances, giving him a comfortable life and the interest of his own club in Bolton, has something to do with it too.

I would have to rate Ray Reardon, who won the title six times in eight attempts in the seventies, above Spencer overall because he maintained peak form for a longer period.

He did, though, become a shade complacent and perhaps worked too hard on the exhibition circuit, which is often better for the bank balance than it is for one's game. All of a sudden he wasn't the player that he had been and in the late seventies and early eighties he started to lose to players he had been beating.

Greatly to his credit, he went back to basics, cutting down his exhibitions in favour of serious practice and preparation for tournaments. It is so important these days to be in the right frame of mind for a big event. The matches are all relatively short, so they are a much more intense and nervy proposition than they used to be in the days when players had longer to settle down. Anyway, Reardon fought his was back, only just losing to Alex in the 1982 world final and in the following season winning a couple of big tournaments.

I do not think Ray is quite the potter he was at his peak but in snooker there are ways of making experience count through sound shot selection and shrewd tactics. Conversely, the game's outstanding younger players like Jimmy White, Tony Meo and Tony Knowles, all pot marvellously well but sometimes lose matches that experience will teach them how to win.

The next few years will no doubt see many more fine young players coming through, largely because there are now so many more competitive opportunities at all levels of the game. Someone has worked it out that Steve had played more matches by the time he was twenty-five than I had played in my entire career!

One unexpected bonus late in my career has been the opportunity to play a part in the modest revival of billiards. I won the Junior Professional Championship three times by the time I was twenty-one but didn't play another billiards match for seventeen years. I entered the United Kingdom Professional Billiards Championship in 1951 with no thoughts of winning it but simply because I fancied a game of billiards. When I did win it, I was asked to play Clark McConachy for the World Professional Championship in the first week of September that year.

This was to have been the first match for the championship since 1934, when Walter Lindrum beat my brother Joe for the title in Australia. Lindrum had no desire to come to England again and as Joe had had his work cut out to earn enough in Australia even to get back home, there was no rush of challengers eager to go all the way to Australia, particularly as Lindrum was just about unbeatable anyway.

However, Lindrum relinquished the title in 1950 and McConachy was an obvious claimant to it. Joe would certainly have beaten him at the time but was not interested in playing for the title, so it was decided that Mac would play the UK champion. I objected, though, to playing in the first week of September, which was so early in the season that I felt I couldn't do myself justice after a summer lay-off. John Barrie was drafted in and Mac beat him fairly easily for the title.

He returned to New Zealand as champion and that was the last we heard of the championship until Rex Williams challenged him in 1968. By this time Mac was seventy-three but Rex still had a devil of a job to beat him by only 265 points in a week's match. Rex, nevertheless, returned to England as champion.

In the next twelve years he made four successful defences, one against Bernard Bennett, one against Jack Karnehm and two against Eddie Charlton. The challenge system worked through the challenger taking responsibility for staging the match and offering the champion, Rex, a financial guarantee.

In this period I never went out of my way to set anything up but in June 1980 Jim Williamson, the proprietor of the Northern Snooker Centre, Leeds, obtained sponsorship from Yorkshire Bank for a title match between Rex and myself. I won fairly comfortably in the end, 5978–4452. I made a break of 583, which is the highest in the championship since 1934, and thus I equalled Joe's record of being the only player to win the World Professional championship at both billiards and snooker.

It is only fair to add that there is no comparison

49

between the standard of play when Joe won the billiards title and the standard when I did. In the early thirties, the top players were playing billiards day in, day out and were frequently making breaks of a thousand or more. When professional billiards collapsed as a public entertainment, professionals concentrated on snooker and turned to billiards only very occasionally. Curiously enough, the deterioration of standard which has inevitably set in has helped make billiards more acceptable again. At least we don't make it boring through never missing!

Later that year, the championship was staged again on a tournament basis – a notable step forward – and I retained the title by beating Mark Wildman in the final. In 1982, I lost by four points to Rex in the semi-final, the closest ever finish in the history of the championship, and he went on to win the title both this year and in 1983, when I was the losing finalist.

It would have been nice to win but if I have played all this time without learning to be philosophical about losing or not playing to the standard I think I should be playing to, there would be something badly wrong. Pleasant as it always is to be paid, I still enjoy the tournaments for their amateur-style satisfactions: the enjoyment of competing and the pleasure in continuing to meet the people involved in the game – players, referees, enthusiasts – whom I have known for years and whom I would otherwise lose contact with.

I cannot see billiards achieving anything like the following there is for snooker but I would like to think it will survive in a minor way. It is a beautiful game, with its own rhythm and satisfactions, but the drama which snooker provides as each frame reaches a climax is seen in billiards more rarely. It is also true that much of the art of billiards is subtle and concealed so the general public cannot respond as they do to snooker's more conspicuous skills. For these reasons, billiards is probably more of a player's than a spectator's game and it is one which I certainly intend to go on enjoying.

Snooker, now, is in the best state it has ever known. Many aspects of its organisation and administration are a long way from perfect but there are more good players than ever before and, through television and sponsorship, greatly increased public interest. I myself enjoy playing more than ever I did and as long as I can give a reasonable account of myself I shall keep trying my hardest. Whatever standard you may be, enjoyment and the satisfaction of doing your best are what the game is really about.

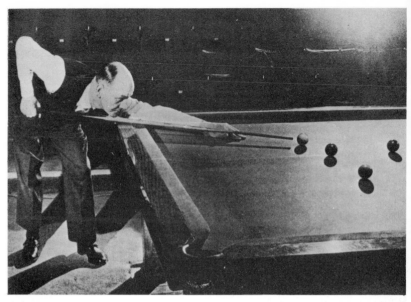

Walter Donaldson, with whom I had many great World Championship battles in the 1940s and 1950s.

World Professional Billiards champion Rex Williams with whom I spent many happy times on the exhibition circuit.

John Pulman, another frequent opponent, shows here a firm, steady bridge as he plays over an intervening ball.

Ray Reardon, six times World Professional champion

John Spencer, three times World Professional Snooker Champion.

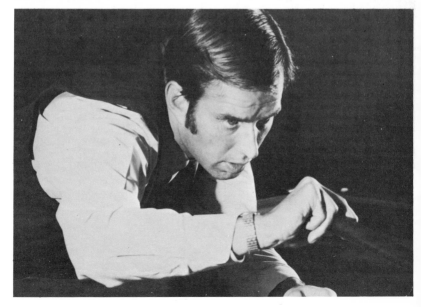

Alex Higgins, World Professional champion 1972 and 1982

Eddie Charlton, the dour Australian who possesses one of the truest cue actions in the game.

Cliff Thorburn, 1983 Benson & Hedges champion

Joe Davis in play.

I congratulate Perrie Mans on his victory over me in the semi-final of the 1978 Embassy World Professional Championship.

Doug Mountjoy, Woodpecker Welsh Professional champion 1980
and 1982

Terry Griffiths, 1982 Coral United Kingdom champion

Steve Davis and Terry Griffiths, who met in five consecutive finals
in the 1982–3 season

Steve Davis in play in regaining the Embassy World
Championship in 1983

Tony Meo, co-winner with Steve Davis of the 1982 Hofmeister
World Doubles

Kirk Stevens, 1983 Canadian Professional champion

Tony Knowles, winner of the 1982 Jameson International

The author — with contact lenses!

The author at the Yamaha Organs Tournament

Part 2
How To Improve Your Snooker

3   You Can Always Improve

Middle aged snooker players are the Micawbers of the sporting world. They are always hoping that something will happen to their style of play which will make them a black or two better. I have, in fact, helped a number of men aged over fifty to play better, and there are some who will say they are even playing better now than they did twenty years ago! This is not as surprising to me as it may be to you, because I know the reason: I was able to point out faults in their stance or action which they had never been aware of. Quite small alterations to stance, for instance, will immediately make a player feel more comfortable and enable him to keep his cue on the line.

It has yet to be proved that age really matters at all in snooker, beyond the pure fatigue of standing up for a dozen stiff frames a day in championships. I know that some whose snooker is not what it was can be heard to plead that their eyesight is not so good – "can't see 'em so well." To me, that is nonsense. I couldn't see them so well in my early twenties, but I had an adjustment made to my spectacle frames and wore glasses for forty years until I switched to contact lenses in 1977.

Still, to the hard-working office type, whose brain is active five days a week and whose digestion perhaps is not what it was, some falling off is likely. What is to be done? First, I suggest, is to recognise that your eyesight is not to blame, or if it is to do something about it. Second, you may find that the main trouble is deterioration in your powers of co-ordination. In short, the timing is no longer so sweet. You tend to hurry to get the actual shot over or you come up on the stroke. The faults which you always made are now worse, too. The trivial things, such as too tight a grip, or a sloppy bridge, or that all too flowing swing, are exaggerated. You worry about your failures.

Well, Doctor Fred Davis doesn't get any younger either. So I can prescribe with first-hand knowledge on the disease of gradual ageing. My prescription is twofold. Chiefly, you must learn to play within your powers. Don't play when you are tired. Don't play too many frames without a rest. And when you rest, even while your opponent is in a break, relax! Don't play as if life itself depended on winning, for that creates tension, which is fatal to timing. Also, try to discover for yourself a more leisurely technique. By this I mean that, without being careless, you should move casually to your stroke, avoid the shots you are quite sure you won't bring off, play for snookers when you know that for you that is better than the bravado type of attempt at potting, and generally use your head like the cunning old fox.

The second piece of advice is to get a good player to play a frame with you and tell you afterwards, quite frankly, why you are missing them. Often, you'll be astonished at the advice he will give you. He will see things, tell you things, he has known about your play for years perhaps. It's a curious thing that although in golf anyone will offer you advice gratis and unasked, in snooker no one ever tells you unless you ask. Best of all, of course, is to have a couple of sessions with a professional. Any ordinary player – and I don't care how bad or how old he is – will benefit from a lesson from a pro and do so practically at once.

There is also this matter of getting the chin down to the cue. Perhaps owing to your maturing build, you now find this very difficult. If so, don't try. That great little Canadian, George Chenier, who was here in 1950, played with a semi-upright stance, almost like the style of old John Roberts at the turn of the century, yet he made a break of 144 which was then the world's record. True, he afterwards adopted the English style, but I doubt if he played better as a result. He proved that it isn't necessary to get the chin down to cue level to play brilliant snooker. So why should you force yourself into a position which is a strain?

Even if you are in your fifties, you have a lot of good snooker in you yet, if you take it easy!

4   The Classic Style

I can just remember the billiards of Melbourne Inman and Tom Reece, those giants of the game, and bitter foes from about 1905 until the advent of big tournament snooker. Inman was champion and a grim, dogged, sometimes cynical fighter. Reece, the Lancashire man, was a beautifully delicate break maker, an infinitely better billiards player from the spectator's point of view. But Reece could rarely beat Inman. Something always happened at the critical point of the match.

They both had styles in which many billiards players performed, and still perform. Inman, a little man, had a long flowing action. When playing from the baulk end to the other end of the table he would follow through so far that his cue rattled on the cushion rail. He believed in length of swing. The cue was taken back perhaps as much as nine inches, and pushed through after impact as much as eighteen inches and more. He was sadly lacking, at top level, in three ball control and was constantly fighting his way out of trouble during a break. Reece, though a much more powerfully built man, (he was at one time a first-class swimmer) was adept at the close cannon. It was a joy to watch him. He held the cue with feathery lightness, and he teased the balls with pure artistry into a series of positions. Maybe he was too artistic.

Today, in the clubs, you will see many players with the long Inman swing, and you will also see many others with the fingertip grip. But today you will not see any professional snooker (or billiards) player with a style anything like either of these great men of a lost generation. The modern grip is firm, and the modern action is short. We have come to realise that, to pot a ball, you have to get your contact between one ball and the other on the exact spot on the object ball. But in making a billiards cannon, you have virtually three widths of a ball as the striking area, because contact on either extreme edge of the second object is enough to score. Therefore far more accuracy of line is essential in snooker than it is in billiards – that is, to make a single successful stroke, not to make a big break.

Inaccuracy can be caused by many things but it comes mostly from inability of the cueing hand to keep on the track which the eye has asked for. Either because the elbow is not right behind the track, or the cue-hand wanders outwards or inwards, or dips up and down, the cue does not go on the right line and the pot is therefore missed. Most, if not all, the errors arising in this way are due to taking the cue-hand backwards out of line, thus causing a swing or arc in the movement. It follows that the shorter the distance of the back movement, the lesser possibility there is of this arc being set up.

Before the war, when I was just coming into top class snooker, I think Joe and I had the shortest of back actions. It was, perhaps, five inches, as against an average of twice that distance. Subsequently, we both cut this down. My own, which is probably the shortest anywhere, is little more than an inch, unless I need a power shot. My preliminary 'waggles' are about an inch or two inches and the cue movement in actual striking is no more. Only the length of the follow through remains. It is still just as important to have a good follow through as ever it was.

In shots requiring some force, such as potting a ball which is almost a full ball contact and adding enough to make the ball run on and round the table, the back action must necessarily be longer. In this case, the follow through must be longer still. Many players fail at power shots because they do not follow through enough. If it's necessary, and possible, I will push the cue through in the direction of the line of the pot as much as three feet.

To play with such a short back movement requires some practice. You have to acquire a new rhythm, or you will find yourself snatching at the shot. But it is something well worth trying. In shortening the movement, remember to hesitate the tiniest fraction before striking. This will give you the necessary slowed-up tempo. Grip firmly, but don't clutch; and let the movement be of the forearm and not of the wrist.

5 One-eyed or Two-eyed Sighting

No one potted more accurately and more consistently than Joe. This was largely because of his ramrod straight cue action backed by the most amazing concentration and consistency. But I did sometimes wonder whether his method of sighting had anything to do with it. Joe always had a weak right eye, and for that reason put his chin practically across the cue in order to sight with the left eye. Most of us sight two-eyed. He sighted one-eyed. I thought to myself more than once, "It's quite possible the old fox has an advantage over us here."

After all, there are many mysteries about sighting. One is the odd fact that in potting there are some angled pots which refuse to correspond to what appears to be the correct line. It could be, for instance, cutting the black into a top pocket from a position near the other top pocket. You find, despite the utmost care in sighting and striking, that you persistently overcut or undercut. Finally, you allow for your own 'error'. To me, to Joe and to all top players there are many such shots on the table which have to be memorised, because they do not seem to be 'according to Euclid'. Why should this be so?

Another mystery lies in the fact that I can pot balls more easily when they are angled into a right hand top pocket than I can those angled into the left hand pockets. When I have asked other players, they have found a corresponding experience. I should expect that a left-handed player would find he pots better towards the left side of the table when the object-ball has to be cut that way.

Only in recent years, apparently, has it been discovered that every person has what you might call a 'sighting eye' and that this can be the right eye or the left eye. The other eye is a sort of auxiliary, which adds strength to the vision and brings the object into focus. (This explains why Graham Miles, twice 'Pot Black' champion, has his cue running so far to the left side of his chin that it ends up almost under his ear.) Now I am in deep water, and I must say that I am only handing on what I am told by an expert. To find your sighting eye, hold up a finger vertically at arm's length, so that it is dead in line with, say, a post. Holding the arm absolutely still, close the right eye and then open it and close the left eye. You will find that one of your eyes is sighting dead on the post, but that the other throws the finger to one side of the post. By this means you know whether you are right-eyed or left-eyed, the accurate one being, of course, the sighting eye and the other the focussing eye. In other words, the sighting eye is the one you would use naturally to look through a telescope. If you wear glasses then of course you must remove them for this test for the lenses are correcting your vision.

What happens when you have made this test? Well, imagine for example that you are a left-handed snooker player, and that you have a particularly narrow stance, one foot practically in front of the other – as many have. That means that you are sighting with your right eye, since you can't face one direction and turn the head in the other without a good deal of physical discomfort. Now, if you also happen to be an erratic and poorish player and despite your keenness and practice you never seem to get any degree of consistency of potting, it could be that you are left-eyed, possibly pronouncedly so.

There could be other reasons, of course, to keep you

back. But if a man is normal physically, not unduly nervous and very keen on improving, he most certainly ought to improve, and to go on improving. Experience and common sense will tell him in time if his stance is wrong or his swing is too fast. He will know if he suffers from the 'jump'. Gradually, he should gain in confidence, which plays a far larger part than most people realise. Gradually his handicap should come down. But you know as well as I do that the majority of regular players in any club stay on their mark all their playing lives. The handicap list shows few changes from year to year, and most of those are among young players or players who have only taken up snooker recently.

It makes me wonder just how many players are sighting with the 'non-sighting' eye. I know that potting is only part of the game, but until you are certain of your potting you cannot hope to tackle positional play, screw and stun. Also, what about those club players who lack confidence in potting but lay snookers exceptionally well? Isn't it true that snookering demands less accurate sighting than potting? Of course it is.

Well, you say, suppose I am sighting one-eyed and with the wrong eye? Yes, that's the problem. If you are dissatisfied with your potting I suggest you experiment. Adopt a squarer stance, to begin with, so that you are sighting two-eyed. You might try sighting with the other eye, even at the expense of a little oddness in the body position. Anyway, at the very worst, you do know the horrible truth about your snooker!

6   The Secret of a Good Player

There are, of course, at least a hundred different 'tips' that can be given by professionals to the ordinary club amateur, all very useful. But it must have occurred to you at some time that all good players have something in common. Isn't it a fact that if you sit in a billiards room and watch two strangers come in to play, you know after seeing a single stroke if one or both happens to be exceptionally good?

You might guess the indicator to be the way a man makes his bridge, spreading long, strong fingers wide and gripping the cloth methodically. True, this is one mark of a good player but I have known amateurs, capable of getting their fifty breaks, who made a bridge like a crab's claw! As to stance, this must depend on the size and shape of the player. Ray Reardon, John Spencer and John Pulman are over six foot. Some have been almost a foot shorter. There have been great players who shape up very narrowly, such as Walter Donaldson, while others are not afraid to let their elbows spread outwards.

But the one thing they all have in common is this: the cue action, which is purely a forearm movement until the ball is struck, is completely divorced from the rest of the body. It is as though the hand and forearm, moving backwards and forwards horizontally, were a single moving part of a machine attached to a solid block. Nothing else moves at all. The bridge fingers remain embedded in the cloth; the head is perfectly still, there is no swaying from the knees, no shifting of the back foot. But the cueing hand is moving even before the player reaches the table and his 'waggles' with the cue are long and rhythmic as he settles into the shot. Then they get shorter until the back stroke of the shot itself is very short, while the follow through is very long. It is all done with a sweet rhythm which you instinctively recognise as 'class' even though the stroke may fail.

The most severe test of your ability to keep the whole of the body quite still comes when you have an awkward stroke to play. For instance, when you have to bridge to play over intervening balls, and raise your bridge hand up to two finger tips – or again, when trying to play at controlled speed directly away from a position tight against a cushion, a downward stroke, glancing the top of the ball; or you might be balancing on one leg. In such cases anxiety alone may create a nervous movement, but the 'great' player nevertheless does succeed in keeping still and striking with a reasonably smooth controlled flow. That, to my mind, is the hallmark of greatness.

How does this concern you, assuming you are a club player of average ability? In this way: if you take the trouble to check up on yourself you will find, without a shadow of doubt, that the great majority of your mistakes are due to movement in some part of your body, or movement of your head, before the stroke is completed. Though it may not perhaps seem so at the time, when you overcut a cut shot – which is very frequently – the reason will be movement somewhere. Whenever you try to force, and fluff a simple pot in doing so, the reason is that you have moved.

In fact, if your tracking is consistent, there is no other reason for most of your mistakes. You can discount the stories of people having a 'marvellous eye' for snooker. Joe had below average eyesight and actually sighted one-eyed for that reason. But it is true, I think, that some take to the game more quickly than others because their nervous impulses or reactions are quieter and more easily controlled. In short, they find it easier to keep still on the stroke and to divorce the forearm action. To you, therefore, in your effort to improve, the first principle must be to get that forearm moving independently and to get the rest of the body anchored so that it will not be influenced. This may not be simple. All nerves, we know, are controlled by the brain and the task of stopping instinctive movement requires quite a bit of conscious effort. You have to remember to stop it. And that's the cause of all the trouble.

How, you will ask, can I explain the success of Alex Higgins, who came from nowhere to win the world title in 1972 and has been among the leading group of players ever since. On the face of it, Alex does everything wrong. He is nervous, jumpy, excitable. He moves on almost every shot he plays. If he did not have extraordinary natural ability he could never get away with it. Even so, if you watch very carefully, you will notice that when Alex is playing well he remains still until a split second *after* he has hit the cue-ball. When he is missing, you can be sure that he has started to move a *fraction before*. He isn't really the exception that proves the rule, though he may appear to be so.

Unless you happen to be a natural snooker genius like Higgins you will find that the more you can keep still at all stages of your stroke the greater dividends it will pay.

7 The Dead Straight Pot

Logically, the straight pot should be easier than the angled pot. It must be so, because you have no worries about guessing or estimating the angle and your target is obvious. Your line of aim is straight through the middle of the cue-ball, through the middle of the object-ball, into the centre of the pocket. What could be easier? Yet one of the commonest remarks in club billiard rooms is, "I knew I'd miss it – I hate dead straight pots." Indeed, among the average and below average players, the angled shot is preferred. The fact is that the average player is off the target with the straight one to the same extent as he is to the angled one, but he forgives himself for missing the angled shot whereas the failure to get the straight one is so glaring a blunder.

This is worth looking into. My own view is that when a player cannot pot a straight ball from a reasonable distance into a fairly open pocket it shows there is something chronically wrong with his cue action. If you watch him closely you will probably discover that his cue never finishes on the line of aim. It is snatched off either to right or left – usually opposite to the pocket – or up into the lampshade.

Taking this a stage further, it also means that the player is moving on the stroke and that he has a bad follow through. Follow through, some people think, is only applied as 'top', to get topspin or 'run' on the ball. But this is totally wrong. Follow through is applied by good players to practically every shot in the game. It is part of the action for two reasons: it ensures, or should ensure, that the cue stays on the line of aim and it also gives rhythm to the action. If the cue is waved to one side after striking the ball, you have no follow through, and you have no certainty that the cue travelled along the line of aim. But if, in the case of the straight pot, you follow through towards the pocket, then as long as your aim is central the object-ball must go in!

Rhythm is a pretty big subject in itself, and I will only say that it is an important part of all ball games, contributing to both timing and co-ordination. It is the secret which enables a slim little man to hit a golf ball three hundred yards and which enables the professional snooker player to screw a ball the length of the table. For the moment we are concerned with getting our straight pot home every time. Going back to the beginning of things, the billiards players of fifty years ago mostly had long flowing actions, long back swings and long follow through. When snooker came, Joe was the first to realise that accuracy of contact must now be even greater. He cut the back swing down to a few inches but he didn't cut the follow through. Cutting the back swing meant less margin for error. The more the cue swings back, the greater the possibility of leaving the true line of travel in coming forward.

If you aim correctly – no problem at all with the straight pot – bring your cue back straight and deliver it through straight you must pot the object-ball. This sort of pot is, in fact, a good one to practise. Set cue-ball and object-ball apart at various distances up to eight or nine feet and drill them in. If you can do this consistently you can reassure yourself that there is nothing wrong with your cue action.

So, coming back to the straight pot, concentrate on keeping the cue dead on line and try to develop a sense of timing.

8   The Mystery of the Cut

A great percentage of pots in snooker are what are called 'cut', which means that the contact is less than half ball. You will find you average from six to ten of these, with the object-ball a foot out from a top pocket and the cue-ball in the baulk area, in every frame. They look easy, because the pocket entrance is wide open, but a great many are missed owing to the distance.

The significant thing about those we miss is that probably over eighty per cent are 'over cut' – that is, played too thinly. With other angled shots, the tendency is always to allow too much 'angle' rather than play too thickly. One answer, of course, is to aim not at the centre of the pocket but at the further angle, thus allowing for your slightly overcutting. A great many players do this. But it is really making one error to rectify another. What is the reason for overcutting? Surely it cannot be that we are, all of us, miscalculating in the same way?

I think you will find the real reason by watching a beginner. When he plays a cut shot his cue, instead of finishing on the line of the shot, ends away in the region of the lampshade, on the side opposite the pocket. He instinctively plays his cue away from the direction of the pocket because his brain is concentrating on side-kicking the object-ball that way.

The good player ends the stroke with the cue going straight through and held firmly on the line. This is difficult and may take years to master but it must be done. Yet even the good player tends to overcut when he misses. He does so, I think, because he has instinctively struck the cue-ball to one side, so applying side without knowing it or else because although his cue action has the perfect finish, something happened during the shot which had the same effect. In short, the psychological effect of the pocket itself is liable to affect all of us. It is worth any snooker player considering this, for if you can eliminate the tendency to overcut, and can be sure of driving the ball well and truly on the line you intend, your potting must at once improve enormously.

One of the most amazing potters of a ball in my experience was the Londoner, Alec Brown, who had to give up when muscular trouble set in, after electrifying audiences in the late 1940s and early 50s. He was smallish, lightly built, a former speedway and track motor cyclist and an engineer. He was only a moderate billiard player, capable of a 200 break or so, but at snooker he potted balls which no other snooker professional would have so much as attempted. Only inferiority in positional play prevented him sweeping the board; as it was, he won several tournaments. Of course, every professional can pot well, or he wouldn't earn a living. Where Alec excelled, and thrilled spectators, was in going for the seemingly impossible, such as cutting a ball three feet down a cushion – and at speed.

Once, when he was asked for his 'secret recipe', something every professional is supposed to have, he said, among other things, that, having sighted his angle and settled into position, he deliberately shut the pocket out of view. Not merely by not looking at it, but by deliberately excluding it. You can do that, you will find, if you concentrate, even with regard to fairly close objects. The result, he said, was that at first you had the feeling of hitting 'into the blue', but the pleasurable sensation when looking up after the shot to find the object-ball had duly disappeared was all the greater.

Certain it is that whenever one is at all anxious over a pot it is difficult to refrain from having 'one eye on the pocket,' and when this happens the result is disastrous. I can't believe, however that that was the whole story so far as Alec's unique genius was concerned. His judgment of the angle, to start with, was astonishing. But I do know amateurs who have adopted his advice with success.

At any rate, when next you play, try to record roughly how many times you miss through overcutting as compared with the times you play too full, and if overcutting is a vice in your play, try giving the pocket the 'blind eye'.

9   Billiards Can Help

Very few snooker players ever practise, and to my way of thinking this is one of the weaknesses of the game. Practising snooker by oneself is a poor form of entertainment and even if the table is 'free' for an odd half hour, the clubman will just sit around and wait for someone to turn up. On the other hand, the billiards player will quite happily set up a position and play by himself for an hour, testing his skill on certain shots like the long jenny, and trying to improve on a break with the red ball only. I suppose the trouble about snooker practice is that you have to be continually taking the balls out of the pocket and spotting them in the same position in order to practise a certain pot; if you don't take this trouble you find yourself idly potting easy ones in pockets all round the table until they are all gone, and then you have to walk round putting them all on the cloth again. That sort of practice is of no value, of course, and no fun either.

To me, practice is really important because I have to keep my standard very high to stay in the company of the small handful of players at the top. But I try not to be bored by it. A great deal of my snooker practice is actually practice at billiards. I take the cue-ball and one red only, and play a hazard game. That is to say, I put the red somewhere around a centre pocket, start from hand, and play for centre pocket in-offs, top pocket in-offs if I must, varied when position is slipping by a pot and then maybe an in-off at the spot end to get back to centre pocket in-offs again. This I find of great benefit. Billiards is essentially a relaxing game compared with snooker, and a series of in-offs (what used to be called losing hazards) cultivates rhythm in the action, combined with practice of follow through and development of a feeling for correct strength to calculate the distance the cue-ball has to run. For the most part, one does not bother with stun, screw or side but plays plain-ball billiards. All this is very good for the snooker player.

Another point in favour of billiards for practice is that probably nine out of ten snooker players at the present time have never even played the game. Among older men in an average club there are some who played a few games of billiards twenty-five years ago, but the present generation of players has no idea at all what the game is like. Well, if you are one of these, let me tell you that, in the first place, with all your skill at snooker, when you find yourself for the first time with two white balls and one red and the rules of billiards to play to, you will be a cruder novice at this game than you ever were at snooker.

Joe was world champion at both games and said that snooker demands more accurate potting and therefore requires more concentration than the cannon game of billiards. That I agree with; but it is more difficult, at the start, to make a cannon than to pot a ball, and far more difficult to control the balls to make two consecutive cannons than to pot twice consecutively. Billiards requires sweetness of touch, delicacy of operation, skill in planning and infinite variety. Only two men, Joe and the great Australian, Walter Lindrum, ever got to the end of the game of billiards. They solved every problem except that of human error and that they virtually reduced to nil except in moments of sheer fatigue.

The pity is that billiards went out of fashion. True, the entries for the amateur championship remained fairly good and the top amateur standard throughout the world improved but in this country at any rate, snooker came to monopolise the tables to the extent that billiards became extinct in many places. They say that snooker is more suited to the tempo of these times. But I think the reason for its ousting billiards is that it is, or appears to be, the game at which the beginner can more easily make a show. He is flattered, too, by the occasional four ball break including two blacks, which sends his score rocketing for what may have been quite trivial shots. This may be a bold prophecy but I think billiards is due for a revival. The entry for the 1977–8 English Amateur Championship was the third highest on record and a few tournaments have sprung up to provide billiards players with the incentive of regular competition, which is vital to any sportsman.

Meanwhile, I am often surprised to see quite good snooker amateurs beaten all ends up by what I should regard as simple snookers. The answer is, of course, that the majority of snooker fans of the present decade have never played billiards at all. You can't play billiards without having some knowledge of angles and the more you play the greater your knowledge becomes. This helps in getting position with the cue-ball using a plain ball shot. The modern snooker player however, wisely uses stun and screw for position and thus his knowledge of the 'throw' of the cue-ball after contact with the object-ball may not amount to much. Cushion shots he never indulges in as snooker does not call for them – at least, until the inevitable happens and the player is snookered. Then, very often, he looks desperately for the angle and fires hopefully at a side cushion.

As to getting out of snookers, I think the chief mistake made is to attempt to use side off a cushion when side is not necessary. Side is almost impossible to calculate exactly, for it depends on the precise point at which the cue-ball is struck. A sixteenth of an inch may make quite a big difference when the cue-ball has to travel three feet to a cushion and three feet back to the ball on. Side also varies according to the speed at which the ball is struck; and the 'throw' from the cushion, when side is used, depends on whether you are playing up table or down. In addition, there is such a thing as slide, by which I mean that if the angle at which you strike the cushion is a thinnish narrow one, you will not get the corresponding angle after hitting the cushion. The cue-ball will 'slide' a bit and if you are using running side it will 'slide' far more.

The safe way is to avoid side if at all possible. To find the correct angle and the point of contact on the cushion, you must stand back and, with your mind's eye, prolong the two sides of your triangle – ie the line to the cushion and the lines from cushion to object-ball – until you are mentally standing in the centre of the base of the triangle, and both imaginary lines are making the same angle to the cushion. Once you get the hang of this it will become relatively easy to work out this piece of mental geometry.

Another thought on snookers; often there are more ways out than one, and you must estimate, first, the easiest, and second the safest. Leave nothing whether you hit the snookered ball or not and be sure not to leave yourself snookered again if you fail – thus giving your opponent the option of a free ball. Frequently there are two alternatives; across the table, or up to the top cushion and back, and you will find more often than not that the longer way round, that is, to the top cushion and back, is the easier.

Two cushion contacts are real billiards, and most snooker fans know little or nothing about them. The fair billiards player knows the exact spot below a top pocket to strike, playing from the centre of the 'D' to bring the cue-ball round the angle, right through the pink spot and back towards the opposite centre pocket. Only by experience, bitter experience, does your modern snooker player learn the centre-pocket in-off trap. The billiards player

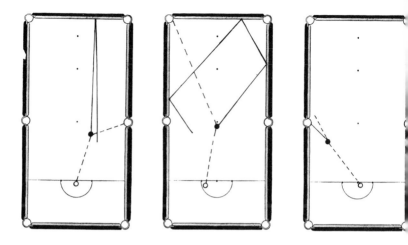

Diagram 1 shows the most basic middle pocket in-off red. The idea is to place the cue-ball in the 'D' at such an angle to the red that a slightly thicker than half-ball contact will take the cue-ball into the pocket and the red up to the top cushion and back again to within an inch or so of its original position.

Diagram 2 shows the sort of shot which may face you if the red drops slightly short of its desired position. As the red has not come far enough for a middle pocket in-off, it is necessary to play the in-off into a top pocket. Spot the cue-ball at such an angle to the red that by playing slightly thicker than half ball you can take the cue-ball into the pocket and bring the red round off three cushions for middle pocket position. The key to success here is to make sure that you strike the cue-ball above centre with a free flowing action with plenty of follow through. You must also avoid using side.

Diagram 3 shows the red having drifted out of position for middle pocket in-offs. Position may be regained here by spotting the cue-ball for an almost full ball pot red in the middle pocket. Play this shot at just the weight to pot the red and take the cue-ball through as shown for what will be a natural half-ball in-off when the red is replaced on its spot.

would never, or should never, be caught by anything so elementary.

Yes, you really ought to start playing a little billiards.

10   Mysteries in the Cloth

Cloths on billiard tables in the clubs I visit vary as much as the turf of cricket wickets. Some are fast, some slow; some are worn and uneven, others are so new that they have almost too much 'grass' on them. But every woollen cloth has this in common – a nap. And that nap can influence the course of the ball quite a lot. It is the nap, for instance, which causes so many mistakes when trying a gentle down-table pot into a middle pocket.

The nap is the surface, like very short brushed wool, and when the cloth is laid and brushed the ball runs *with* the nap from baulk to spot end, and *against* the nap when playing from the spot end towards baulk. Playing against the nap is something like bowling into the wind at cricket, or driving into the wind at golf. The nap exerts a pressure against the ball. If, for instance, you play slowly from one centre pocket to the other, the ball will drift upwards, through the pressure of the nap. Allowing for the nap is necessary in all slow shots played against it, and even in medium pace shots if over four feet or so; but how much to allow must depend on the condition of the cloth and, as I have said, this varies from table to table.

Most errors of the nap are made with centre pocket shots. These problems can be twofold: firstly, if the cue-ball has to travel across the nap and against it for over two and a half feet (for a slow shot), and secondly, if the object-ball has to make a similar journey. The worst combination, therefore, is playing a slow shot with the cue-ball near a top corner pocket and the object-ball a bit south of the pink spot. Try this and you will find that nine times out of ten the object-ball will hit the cushion above the pocket.

Sometimes, a slow shot is essential and when it is, you must make an allowance. It is usually sufficient if you aim to pot your ball against the inside of the lower pocket angle. But the good experienced player tries to avoid the slow shot always. He does this by employing screw or stun or drag. Thus he can send the cue-ball off at a fair speed, defeating the influence of the nap, or at any rate most of it.

The player who is beginning snooker ought to cultivate a forcing style right from the start. Those gentle taps cause more disappointment in the game than one's opponent's flukes. The player sees the black rolling nicely and slowly straight for the corner pocket and then, quite mysteriously, it goes off course. In this case, it may not be the nap, but a hidden grain of chalk or some dust that has permeated beneath the cloth. You are asking too much to expect accuracy and perfection and although on a well kept table you usually get it, even then you will have your failures. Chalk spots on the cue-ball will also cause trouble, as all good billiards players know, for in billiards, the delicate shot cannot be avoided. Compared with billiards, snooker is what old Tom Reece once described as something to be played in clogs. It is a power game.

But this doesn't mean that the basher has any advantage. The power must be controlled. At times great power is needed, as, for instance, when you have to play the full length of the table to pot a dead straight ball which is within an inch of the pocket. Such a shot requires deep screw, and power to sustain the screw until it gets there. It is not an easy shot. But it is the only one, for the slow shot will surely run off the lines, especially if down table.

The shot in which you are tempted to tickle a ball gently into a centre pocket in order to stay on the blue must be played with stun — a sharp contact but not a heavy one — which pulls the ball back and kills its travel. And for a large variety of shots in which you want the cue-ball to slow down rapidly after contact — as, for instance, the long distance snooker — the use of drag is invaluable. The professional makes great use of this, for it enables him to send the ball away at a fair pace which diminishes rapidly after travelling six or nine feet. Cultivate drag, but be very careful that you strike centrally, otherwise you will pull the cue-ball off the line.

Personally, I never give the nap a chance. If I play a medium pace shot into it — let us say, potting brown off its spot into a baulk pocket from a position near the opposite centre pocket — I will allow something, maybe an inch. I never play a crawler if I can find any other stroke to play. If you find it difficult to get out of the habit of these slow shots, get a new cue, weight seventeen ounces and shorter than usual.

11 The Crash Artists

In the early thirties when snooker was beginning to displace billiards in popularity, we were 'invaded' by some Canadian professionals. Clare O'Donnell was one; Conrad Stanbury, who liked it here so much that he never went back, was another. O'Donnell, during a match at Thurston's, where decorum held that players wore evening clothes minus the jacket, turned up in mid-Western style, stripping off his jacket to reveal no waistcoat, and a fine strong leather belt adorned with silver nobs. His clothes, of course, were unimportant. It was the difference in style between the Canadians and our players that created a minor furore.

These visitors played literally every stroke (yes, I mean that) with screw or stun. No matter what the position was, nor what position was sought, the object-ball was crashed into its pocket with a violence that flabbergasted everyone. Our own experts, emerging as they were from a billiards style, were still exploiting dainty touches. Joe, of course, employed the screw—stun game and led the field with ease. But even he never used the force – nor needed to – that these powerful Canadians used. For the record, although they could make their century breaks, they lacked finesse and never made our top class. But the way they could screw a ball was something to remember with awe.

After the Second World War came another Canadian,

George Chenier, a player of altogether higher calibre, who indeed quickly proved to be genuinely world class. Many Canadians made centuries but he made them in top company. He also showed unusual skill at screw and stun without walloping the ball like his predecessors. In the last five years, the current Canadian champion, Cliff Thorburn, who reached the world professional final in 1977, has emerged as a world class player through his sound methodical technique and excellent concentration.

I toured Canada in 1958 for a series of matches, including a big one with Chenier in Vancouver, a most amiable chap and ideal to tour with. I played before the biggest audiences I had ever seen for snooker. My first shock came when I discovered that in Canada they used what was known as the 'Imperial' ball which was a lighter ball than our own Crystalate, for though the size of the ball is officially prescribed the weight is not. I found that with the Canadian weight the screw shot was much easier but the follow through action was much more difficult, if not downright impossible. The effect, when playing for follow through, was that the cue-ball tended to jump. This was most disconcerting, as you can imagine, for in England every good player cultivated follow through for a great number of positional ploys, particularly when in a break at the spot end. To pot black and have the cue-ball run through and around two cushion for the next red is one of the standard strokes. But to do this you must use strong follow through. Curiously enough, when the lighter Super Crystalate ball replaced the Crystalate ball in 1973 much the same problems were encountered.

In that situation, it was possible to play deep screws I would scarcely have attempted at home, but in the early stages of the match the balance was very much against me, and at one time I was trailing by eight frames, a position nearly always fatal against such an experienced player as Chenier. However, I saw at once that I must adopt a different technique — not so easy as it sounds. At every stroke in a break I had to remember that my next position must be one where I could use stun or screw, or, at any rate, avoid follow through. I worked steadily to a plan and won the match. In my tour of six weeks, playing with the lighter balls, I made nineteen century breaks, which at that time was very nearly a record. It was certainly a very good performance by any standard and I quote it only to demonstrate that playing with 'Imperials' was actually easier.

Incidentally, this experience explained why the Canadians whom we had seen were such forceful players. To them screw and stun were the only practical means of positional play, and when they found our heavier ball did not respond so dynamically, they walloped it harder. I'll say this for them, too; their cue action must have been miraculously true, for the harder you hit the more likely you are to miss the pot. It reminds me that when I was working hard at the game I was once told, "When playing screw or stun, try to think of the cue-ball as a wall, through which you intend to drive your cue. Don't think of it as something that moves but as something stationary and heavy."

Of course, there is far more than this in playing screw shots, but if you are a young or an ambitious player who tends to avoid screw because it so often leads to missing the pot, just think that if you had always played every shot with screw and stun you would have learnt to pot that way. I don't advise the mid-Western wallop, far from it, but I do recommend that you always take the firm shot where there is a preference. Screw is the heart of modern snooker, all the more so since the change to Super Crystalate balls.

12   The Tall Man

One of the complaints most often made is that the billiards table was originally designed for little men. The height from floor to cushion rail is laid down as between 2'9½" and 2'10½", and I remember thinking when I was playing John Pulman how justifiable this complaint was. Pulman stands 6'2".

Before Pulman, Ray Reardon and John Spencer, leading players tended to be short fellows: Walter Lindrum, Melbourne Inman, Willie Smith, for instance. Joe was and I am less than medium height. Travelling back into history, one comes to the man who was one of the most consistent potters the game has ever known: W J Peall. Before the spot-barred days of billiards (when the player could pot the red off the spot as often as he pleased) Peall won some games of 600 up without his opponent playing a stroke. He cut the cut into the top pocket from hand and then potted the red into the top pockets until he ran out unfinished. Peall stood 4'10" and wore false heels.

In the old days, only the great John Roberts Jnr, among the top sawyers, was a tall man. He, of course, played billiards only; moreover, in those days all players had a semi-upright stance, and the present potting theory of rifle sighting, with the chin practically touching the cue, was unknown. The biggest man I can remember in the professional game was John Barrie, perhaps half an inch taller than Pulman. Joe thought Barrie would be a world champion and, but for a recurrent depressive condition which put him out of the competitive game for twenty years until he made a comeback recently, he could well have come close to that. But he always gave the impression of being much too big for the table. He seemed to be worried about where to put his hind part when stooping down to get his chin behind the ball and his stance was a curiously twisted one in which he stowed the rear portion sideways, out of the way as it were, so that his cueing arm could travel freely.

In amateur circles one sees tall men in the same difficulty. Some face it by spreading their legs very wide apart in the form of the base of a tripod, and then sitting back on their haunches. This looks unsound and probably is. Pulman contrives to beat this difficulty very gracefully. True, his hind part is up in the air, describing a semi-circle like the neck of a swan; but he manages with a reasonable stance of not more than fifteen inches between his feet, and he faces half right in the orthodox manner. It seems a physical miracle when you think about it. I think his secret, however, is that although the stance is that of a short man, his weight distribution is different. Whereas the experts advocate that a player should lean forward with the weight over the front knee, Pulman's weight is a trifle further back. His back leg is very stiff and well anchored, and it is practically vertical. I think his weight is mainly on that vertical back leg. This is a very different thing from sitting on one's haunches, or of leaning backwards. Pulman's cue is quite short and when he bends down he does so without difficulty, with his cue hand slightly in front of the line down from the elbow – a good thing, which I do myself. His action is economical, and his strength gives him an enviable range of power. All tall men should see Pulman play, if they get an opportunity. They should study him and find out why and how he masters the disadvantage of his height with such apparent ease.

Big men do not have all the bad luck, however. Their extra reach is a very real advantage. I have watched Pulman, who also has big hands, reaching across the table to bridge over intervening balls and make a pot comfortably, whereas I should have to take the long spider, a fearsome implement in itself, playing the stroke gingerly and at considerable risk.

Having played Pulman a great deal in the 1950s and early 60s, usually over three days or a week, I have had ample time to study his technique. I have not played John Spencer so much and have therefore not dissected his stance in the same way except to realise immediately that he looks more comfortable in his stance than any other tall man I have ever seen. His secret lies, I think, in being exceptionally flexible in the waist and hips. He does not carry much weight, so even though he does not play with his feet very far apart, he always looks perfectly balanced and comfortable.

Ray Reardon, who is also over six foot, to my eyes looks more awkward at the table, though this may be due to the way he plays with his elbow jutting out instead of being above the cue in the more conventional way. He is a player who keeps himself fit and at a proper fighting weight and always seems able to fold himself into the various awkward positions which crop up from time to time when it is necessary to bridge over a ball or go to the verge of over-reaching rather than use the rest or half-butt. Ray seems to have a very strong back, which sometimes makes his stance assume the shape almost of an inverted 'L'. To me, it looks uncomfortable but it obviously hasn't proved uncomfortable enough to prevent him winning six world titles.

Snooker apart, most short men would have preferred to be tall and I don't think tall men would have exchanged their stature for anything less. So if we little 'uns do have an advantage at the billiard table, well, go and play cricket. Only one point about all this leaves an uneasy thought: the figures produced by medical authorities annually show that our offspring tend to grow bigger each decade. In the near future we shall have a race of six-footers with a sprinkling of six foot sixers and an occasional seven footer, and what is going to happen then? Maybe the answer lies in a story told by Joe of a table he played on in a mining town in South Africa, where, owing to a subsidence, the whole township was on a slope. The club he played in had suffered similarly, and the table legs were consequently six inches longer at one end than at the other.

13   The Safety-First Fiend

You find him in every club billiards room. He isn't a very good player, but he takes a long time to beat because he plays so many safety shots. When facing someone of his own class, the frame takes forty-five minutes or more to finish – sometimes ten minutes go by before the first red goes down, and if the game is still 'alive' on the pink it can be another ten minutes before the vital colour is in a pocket. Then everyone sighs with relief at the end of a long and boring game and there is a rush for cues by those who have been waiting patiently for the table.

There is another type of safety-first fiend. He is quite a useful performer, and loves to lay devilish snookers. When the game is wide open for him so that there is no excuse whatever for snooker, he shows himself to be a deadly potter and one wonders why he so often refuses to 'have a go' when a good opening comes along. But one admires him far more than the other safety-first type because he is playing really good snooker.

The problem is, first of all, to decide how much snookering is advisable, as a means of winning. Nothing else matters very much. There are still places in this country where it is considered bad form to snooker unless you are in dire need of points to catch your opponent. This is nonsense, of course, for snookering is the big idea which distinguishes the game from a mere test of potting, such as pyramids used to be. It is the instrument which gives the player behind on his points a chance of winning. It is true that in all clubs players are likely to be irritated when their opponents keep them tied down in the long grass for stroke after stroke, and one hears many a sarcastic remark about 'getting on with the game' and about persons unnamed who are afraid to leave anything. All this should be ignored. If your chance of winning will improve by laying a snooker, lay it – with a smile.

But it is my experience that the player in any grade who overdoes safety play does not do himself justice. He loses games and matches he could have won with bolder policy. This goes for professionals and extends right down the line to novices. The moderate players who fall into the safety habit will very rarely improve, for the simple reason that they are playing negative stuff instead of strengthening their style by going out for well planned strokes. If you're a moderate player and your opposition is on much the same level, consider this: suppose you go right through a frame without a single safety stroke or do not attempt a snooker until the closing stages, and only then if you need a snooker to win – you may let your opponent in with a good position, but how often will he profit by it? Like you, he often misses easy ones, and in fact he is far more likely to leave you something when you force him to try to pot than when you don't.

In ordinary club snooker, after the first few sparring shots to loosen the pack, the players ought not to think of playing safe, but should go out for constructive attack all the way. They should act like great batsmen, who are always looking for runs. Letting the other fellow in should be completely forgotten at this stage. That is the only way to raise your standard and it also happens to be the best way to win. Forcing the opponent on to the defensive is a good sign. If he sees you are potting well and plays safe, remember he himself cannot score. Too much safety play seems to stultify potting skill. When the opening comes, the safety player can't get the easy one down.

In most snooker matches of a serious character, safety play tends to dominate whenever the opponents are of equal ability. Each is naturally cautious and anxious to prevent the other getting away with a sizeable break, and this tends to slow down the play somewhat. Professionals are affected in the same way in important matches. It is something you have to fight against, for it is a fact that you can't win matches by non-scoring. The ideal is to play an aggressive game at all times, without being rash. Go out for pots, even very difficult ones, if you can calculate that in the event of getting the red down you will be on a colour, and that if you fail, you won't leave a sitter. And if forced to play safe because there is nothing on, use your imagination and your knowledge of angles, and try to make it a really difficult snooker.

Only by attempting the difficult combination of pot and position at every opportunity will you improve. Very often it happens that the cue-ball is near the top cushion, with no ball pottable direct, and you have to seek shelter in the long grass in baulk. But even so you can often do this just as easily by playing a corner pocket double. This is always a tricky shot, but it can be a shot to nothing, and it is an opening for both pot and position even if the position is below the brown. Practice makes perfect at doubles, as with everything else in snooker, and as few players ever have any solo practice, the next best thing is to practise off a safety shot during play.

My last remark about safety play echoes my first: resolve that you won't be the billiard room bore who keeps the game dragging on interminably by pokey, meaningless, ineffectual safety shots. Have a go, Joe! And enjoy your snooker.

14   The Man Who Wins Matches

Most clubs run an annual handicap tournament on knock-out lines. Usually the favourite is the scratch man and the 'wise' money goes on those members who have been playing only a year or two but have made such headway that the handicapping committee have not caught up with them.

I cannot tell you how to win a tournament, but there are points which will help most players in their individual matches. If it is the sort of club in which most competitors play in perhaps only one tournament during the year, the occasion, when it comes, is quite formidable. The cloth is brushed, the pyramid never looked quite so professional, the seats around are filled, and there you are, with your opponent shaking hands and the referee, very much on his toes, organising the scoreboard and telling you to toss for choice of breaking off. You win, you decide (I hope) to break off, and you remember too late that too thick a contact will most probably bring the cue-ball down towards the blue and a red also comes down invitingly near the centre pocket. Your opponent is in with an easy red and blue already!

Many of these handicap heats are settled in the first few minutes, largely because both players are rather nervous, both are liable to make errors of which they are ashamed and the player who settles down first may, with a bit of luck, get a winning advantage quite soon. Meanwhile, his luckless opponent gets worse, tells his friends he can't understand his own bad form, and settles into a groove of safety play from which he can never hope to catch his man.

Briefly, the man who relaxes first has a very big advantage. Tension sets up all manner of errors, such as 'head up', stabbing, holding the cue too tightly, moving the feet, playing hurriedly and hitting too hard. The secret of relaxing is by no means easy. But it does make sense. You will avoid tension, for instance, if you arrive in plenty of time for the match and settle down to a cup of coffee or a modest drink at your leisure. Between shots you should force yourself to relax, mentally and physically; mentally, by watching the game with a studious but quite detached mind, and physically by releasing that fierce clutch on the cue, standing easily and breathing long and deep.

In the course of play, the secret is to follow your normal pattern of play. Most are tempted to play fast and slapdash and others to be over-deliberate. When I began in tournaments I was a very slow player. It took me longer than most to make up my mind as to my shot and my action was also slow. This is wrong, though not so wrong as playing too fast. It's the natural tempo which you must find and this of course varies from player to player. Willie Smith, at seventy, was still racing round the table like an excited two-year-old pony, but that was his tempo. If he had had to play slower he'd have been utterly miserable and unable to do himself justice.

Apart from tension, tactics enter very largely into match play on handicap. The long handicap player hesitates to go for a red which looks difficult, finally does so, plays nervously, and leaves it on, which was the very thing he told himself not to do against the crack opponent. He should try to play naturally and within his powers. Always playing for safety must result in being beaten – it also sets up a chronic inferiority complex in the safety player and just the reverse in his opponent!

Don't go for shots which you normally fail at, just because a crowd is watching, but when you do go for a pot, do so with a single thought – to get it down and leave good position on a colour. If any fear creeps in you will surely miss.

One other point about club competitions: the referee. He is usually a well-meaning fellow member, but sometimes he is over keen and an awful nuisance. The referee should try to efface himself as much as possible, not dominate the room. I have often suffered from the chummy type who will stand so close to see if I foul that he is literally breathing down my neck. He means well, but he's a pest! The ideal referee makes no remarks, calls the score regularly, is always ready with the rest, and stands well away in the shadows with an ever watchful eye. He also knows the rules.

15 Can You See Properly?

There was a minor sensation in the snooker world when I played in London, at Thurston's in Leicester Square, a year or two before the war. Not because I was the younger brother of Joe, the champion, but because I wore glasses. No one of any repute in snooker wore glasses; yet here was I, a professional, playing in the world's most important tournament with spectacles. Of course, innumerable inquiries followed, and these became even more numerous as I achieved a measure of success. Subsequently, many professionals played in glasses as well as a great many amateurs at all levels. Somewhat late in life I changed to contact lenses, which are even better, but they are not everyone's cup of tea.

Let me go back a bit. I was a young man in Chesterfield, watching from afar my illustrious brother Joe tearing up the opposition. My own game was good, both at billiards and snooker, but just when I was contemplating making a bid for fame in London my sight began to fail. The balls took on a woolly edge. So it seemed that, at the age of twenty or so, my career was over before it had started. The story runs that Joe asked me what was going wrong, that I said I couldn't see properly and he retorted, "Well, get some glasses!" It wasn't quite like that, because in those days wearing glasses would have been fatal to snooker. He suggested an eye test.

Out of the discussions that followed came a pair of glasses fitted with an angling joint. This does not affect the angle of the lens and it enables one to push the rim up out of the line of sight. As all players who use spectacles have found out, the upper part of the rim cuts off the distant part of the table unless the player raises his head to a half-upright position. My angling joint, worked out by Theodore Hamblin of Wigmore Street, London, made this unnecessary.

With my spectacles, I was still only twenty-six when, in the season of 1939–40, I met Joe in the final of the World Championship, gave him as stiff a fight as he had ever had, and set the world record championship break (at that time) of 113. With ordinary spectacles or no spectacles at all this could not possibly have happened. I think there must be hundreds of thousands of keen snooker players who have suffered from that top rim. The answer is very simple and I think it probable that all opticians can fix your spectacles in a similar way. In fact, as snooker has become more popular such swivel-lens spectacles have become more common. I don't promise you will become a champion, but your snooker should improve and your pleasure increase enormously once you no longer have to squint and tilt your head unnaturally.

16   Snooker's Gadgets

In every game and sport, sooner or later, the inventive-minded folk get to work to make it easier to play well. In golf we have had manufacturers making balls which fly farther and farther, a club which is said to keep them straighter, a putter to slot the ball into the hole better, and, I remember, a harness to keep the head down! In athletics, there have been shoes with a high springy heel for the high jump and of course the fibre-glass pole for the pole vault.

I remember someone inventing a new type of rest for snooker which, it was claimed, would render potting quite simple. It was far from being the first attempt at this idea. I recall an invention of a double ring. The lower part fitted round the first finger of the bridge hand and the cue went through the upper ring, the idea being that the cue was thus more or less fixed in its channel. Subject to risking breaking your finger, it was said, you couldn't fail to push the cue along the line of aim. All you had to do was to aim correctly, and this double ring did the rest.

It need hardly be pointed out that if such gadgets did what they were intended to do they would be barred at once. This was the case during a *Daily Mail* Gold Cup snooker match at Thurston's just before the war. Alec Brown, one of the most devastating potters the game has ever known, produced his own 'secret weapon' during his match with the late Tom Newman when, after potting a red, he found the cue-ball in the middle of the pack. To cue it at all would have been immensely difficult, if not impossible, as the rest could not be positioned anywhere behind it. He then produced what became known as the 'fountain pen cue' from his breast pocket, where he carried it beside his fountain pen. It was a miniature cue, a few inches in length, with a proper tip on it. He just leaned over from the top end and stroked the cue-ball gently towards him onto the black. Amid the hubbub, Charlie Chambers, the referee, asked to examine the miniature cue. After a thoughtful interval he merely said, "Foul, seven away" and put seven points onto Newman's score. Later he said he had decided the 'cue' was not an implement customarily used in the game and this shrewd decision was later upheld by the Control Council. It is now stipulated that a cue must be at least three feet in length and must not depart from conventional shape.

Professionals are always being asked where they get their tips. Players think there is something special about them because the screwing power the professional can exert baffles him. But we are all on the look-out, always, for good tips, and it is impossible to tell until after use whether a new tip is likely to be good or bad. And, of course, there is much more satisfaction in getting results by good style. Better than looking for a gadget to make potting easier is to find out why you find it so difficult. A great many moderate players make such a bad bridge that even with that double ring they would be no better off, because the bridge hand would wobble. Few realise what great benefit comes from a really firm, tenacious bridge. Leading players hold the cloth so tensely with their fingerpads that they stretch the cloth.

Making a good bridge is quite easy. Place the hand flat on the table with fingers straight and spread widely. Then, keeping the fingers straight from base knuckle to top, draw the pads inwards. You should now have a pronounced hump with rigid sides. Cock the thumb to make the channel and keep the pads well down so that they grip the cloth. Now your bridge hand is immovable.

To this you can make one useful addition, unless the position of the cue-ball renders it impossible, and this is to keep the whole of the cueing arm also straight. This has a side effect: it braces the opposite shoulder back and it is in this position that you will find the cue now going back and forth easily and freely, quite detached in movement. And that is the ideal. It is a habit of many a top player that, as he approaches the table, he runs one hand up and down the cue and braces his shoulders. The hand movement is instinctive preparation for free swinging, and the shoulder bracing for the stance he knows he will adopt.

I don't undertake that this will cure all your faults. You may be jumping on the shot, or you may be holding the cue out away from the body. What I am quite sure of is that it will cure many of the commonest faults.

17   The Most Thankless Job

Every game has to have its referees, or judges, or umpires, and snooker and billiards are no exceptions in competitions. They do differ from most other games in that practically all friendly games are played without referees or markers and even in competitions some referees do not know the rules thoroughly. In nearly all the thousands of league matches played every weekday night in this country, the games are controlled by another member of the team, a reserve player or by a local club member roped in, perhaps unwillingly, for the evening. There is of course a growing number of properly certified referees who hold either 'C', 'B' or 'A' grade certificates and with many more tournaments about than ever before, refereeing is a splendid way of getting involved in the game if you feel that you are not going to amount to much as a player. Whether you intend to take a referee's examination or not, however, it is very much in your interests to know the rules. Anyone can buy a copy but as the B & SCC jealously protects the copyright you must apply to them in Huddersfield for your copy.

It is a good general rule that the rules of these games are framed for fairness and in the spirit of sportsmanship. This outlook will often settle awkward questions. For instance, the rule is that if a player is snookered he is bound to make a genuine attempt to hit the ball 'on', and he can be disqualified for a deliberate miss or a deliberate foul. Now, it does happen – not often, fortunately – that it is absolutely impossible to hit the ball 'on'. It may be that the last red, completely surrounded by colours, or the cue-ball itself, after potting a red, may have run into the pack and so buried itself that to hit a colour is impossible. When this happens, some purists are inclined to argue that, as the striker is bound to foul, the foul is therefore deliberate, and he must lose the game. But when the point was put to old John Bisset, much criticised in his time but in retrospect the man who held the then B A & C C together as chairman for many years, he said, "In our game we do what is fair and reasonable. It is not reasonable to disqualify a player because the rules literally force him to foul. Therefore, he should be allowed to foul his way out, pay the usual forfeit and let the game go on."

Unfortunately, the rules of snooker are sometimes contradictory. One instance is this: if you are on the last red, and after a foul you have a free ball and select blue, the rules tell you that for the purposes of the stroke the blue is a red. If you pot blue you score one point and you are on a colour. Very good. But another rule says that if, in these circumstances, you happen to miss the blue and hit the red, this is a foul. So the blue is a red for the purpose of scoring, but it is not a red in the sense that all reds are 'on' balls. Very confusing.

The free ball rule causes many problems. It seems simple enough. If snookered by a foul stroke you are entitled to a free ball. Fine – this means you can lay another snooker so long as it is not behind the free ball and this gives you a chance to catch up on the scoreboard. But when only pink and black are left, what happens if you are snookered behind the black by a foul stroke? It used to be the case that you had a free ball, the black, but it was a foul to snooker behind it. Many a player needing a couple of snookers to win at the last vital stage argued bitterly about this aspect of the rules and eventually the rule was changed. This is the only stage of the game where you may snooker behind the nominated ball.

Here is an anomaly: if you pot two reds with the same stroke you score two points, which is logical, but if you are on the yellow, and have a free ball and nominate brown, and in potting brown you also pot yellow, you do not score for two yellows but for one only. This, too, is not understood by many players.

Referees must also call all fouls and if necessary award free balls as they see them, and at once. It's understandable that few players think this is so, because it is necessary at cricket to appeal for catches and for lbw. Why cricket laws should be so framed that a batsman can have a free 'life' legitimately just because the fielding side didn't notice he was out, I cannot understand. This is not the position in snooker and billiards at all. As in football, the referee blows for the fouls he sees; the captain may appeal, and he will, if in doubt, ask his linesmen. In snooker and billiards an appeal for a foul may be made, and the referee may, if he thinks it necessary, ask spectators for their evidence. He isn't bound to accept it, even so.

Of course, the ideal would be for a game to have rules so simple and so well known that it controls itself. The so-called 'play again' rule reduced the number of disputes over rules, though I feel bound to mention that it was introduced by the professionals and for many years bitterly resisted by the B A & C C even to the extent that official recognition of Joe's 147 break, the first ever achieved under match conditions, was initially refused because the professionals were then playing to the 'play again' rule. The rule itself is simple; after any foul, the offender may be requested to play the next stroke.

18 Playing to the Rules

Try your knowledge of the rules of snooker with a few questions:

1   Your opponent fouls, and leaves the cue-ball angled to the last red. What is the procedure?

2   A player is laid a snooker, the last red is over a pocket. He is quite sure he can't hit it and he plays out in another direction so that no free ball is left, but from where his opponent cannot pot the red. What, if any, is the penalty?

3   Striker is on a red, plays it, cue-ball then hits black and goes into a pocket. What is the penalty?

4   Striker is on a red, plays it. Cue-ball then strikes black and pots black. Penalty?

5   Striker has a free ball with one red left. He nominates black, but misses the black and hits the red. Is this a fair stroke?

6   Striker pots a red. Cue-ball comes to rest against blue, touching. Striker nominates blue, plays the ball gently to a snookering position behind black without moving blue. Is this a fair stroke? If not, penalty?

Perhaps you know all the answers. But I will assert that most readers will stumble over half of them.

The thing that strikes me as oddest of all in connection with rules is that local league games, generally fought with real cup-tie spirit, are often refereed by someone whose knowledge of the rules is rough and ready, with no rule book to refer to if a squabble develops. There were cases in the more status conscious 'good old days' in which, out of a mistaken sense of protocol, the chairman of the home club refereed, though he had seldom played.

I have long since come to the conclusion that for the happiness and comfort of all, it would be a grand thing if it was compulsory for every club in every league to keep a rulebook on the premises. This is available from the Billiards and Snooker Control Council, Alexandra Chambers, 32 John William Street, Huddersfield, West Yorks. In purchasing a rule book you will also have the satisfaction of supporting the game in a practical financial way as these sales constitute a significant factor in the B & S C C's revenues. The B & S C C will also tell you the name and address of the local coach and examiner, in case you should wish to take an official certificate and wear the official referees's badge.

Now about those questions, which I chose at random. Here are the answers:

1   You are not entitled to a free ball because you are not snookered. But you may pick your ball up and play from hand (the 'D'). You could also use the 'play again' rule and ask your opponent to play the next stroke – at the red, of course.

2   A deliberate miss is not allowed. The player must try to hit the ball on. If the referee is quite sure the miss was deliberate he may replace the ball(s) to its original position, award the appropriate penalty and order the player to play again. For a second infringement he may award the game to his opponent.

3   Four points

4   Seven points

5   No, you must hit the nominated ball. Penalty four points.

6   Yes, a fair stroke. It would be a foul if blue moved while he played away.

Most players get caught out at one time or another by

some obscure aspect of the rules but the great thing is never to make the same mistake twice. I was caught in 1964 when I challenged John Pulman for the world title he had held unopposed since 1957. It had been eight years since I had played a really serious match. I was a couple of frames in front when I was awarded a free ball. It was obvious which ball I was taking but I was unaware that, however obvious it was, all free balls – unlike colours taken in the normal way – had to be nominated audibly. I failed to do so, the referee called a foul, and this proved to be the turning point of the match. Nowadays, however, you only have to nominate audibly if your choice is not obvious.

You should always, of course, try to learn from experience. If you've lost a match you feel you should have won, try to work out where you have gone wrong. More often than not, it is not through any spectacular play by your opponent but through missing shots yourself that you would normally expect to get. Consistency is perhaps the supreme snooker virtue. Get into the habit of not missing the easy ones and you will find your success rate with the not so easy ones will improve.

Be realistic about your own ability. If you judge yourself by world championship standards you will live in a perpetual state of frustration and disappointment. If you can see yourself as an average league player who is gradually improving, and I hope you are, you will enjoy your successes much more. Never forget that enjoyment is the key to it all. It certainly has been with me.

Championships Records

WORLD PROFESSIONAL

1927	Joe Davis	Tom Dennis	20—11
1928	Joe Davis	Fred Lawrence	16—13
1929	Joe Davis	Tom Dennis	19—14
1930	Joe Davis	Tom Dennis	25—12
1931	Joe Davis	Tom Dennis	25—21
1932	Joe Davis	Clark McConachy	30—19
1933	Joe Davis	Willie Smith	25—18
1934	Joe Davis	Tom Newman	25—23
1935	Joe Davis	Willie Smith	25—20
1936	Joe Davis	Horace Lindrum	34—27
1937	Joe Davis	Horace Lindrum	32—29
1938	Joe Davis	Sidney Smith	37—24
1939	Joe Davis	Sidney Smith	43—30
1940	Joe Davis	Fred Davis	37—36
1941-1945	No contest		
1946	Joe Davis	Horace Lindrum	78—67
1947	Walter Donaldson	Fred Davis	82—63
1948	Fred Davis	Walter Donaldson	84—61
1949	Fred Davis	Walter Donaldson	80—65
1950	Walter Donaldson	Fred Davis	51—46

After the 1951 Championship the professional players disaffiliated from the Billiards Association and Control Council and organised their own World Championship with all the leading players participating. This was recognised in the public eye as the World Professional Championship although the B.A. and C.C. also organised their own official World Championship in which Horace Lindrum beat Clark McConachy, the only other entrant, 94—49.

1952	Fred Davis	Walter Donaldson	38—35
1953	Fred Davis	Walter Donaldson	37—34
1954	Fred Davis	Walter Donaldson	39—21
1955	Fred Davis	John Pulman	37—34
1956	Fred Davis	John Pulman	38—35
1957	John Pulman	Jack Rea	39—34

Fred Davis defeated George Chenier in Vancouver 1958 in a match billed as the World Championship but not officially recognised.

118

No Championships were organised from 1957–1964 when, after a truce with the B.A. and C.C., a new system came into being in which the champion defended his title against a series of single challengers. These matches resulted:

1964	John Pulman	Fred Davis		19—16
1964	John Pulman	Rex Williams		40—33
1965	John Pulman	Fred Davis		37—36
1965	John Pulman	Rex Williams	(matches)	25—22
1965	John Pulman	Fred van Rensburg		39—12
1966	John Pulman	Fred Davis	(matches)	5— 2
1968	John Pulman	Eddie Charlton		39—34

Under a two-year sponsorship from John Player, the Championship reverted to a tournament basis in 1969.

1969	John Spencer	Gary Owen	46—27
1970 (April)	Ray Reardon	John Pulman	39—34
1970 (Nov.)	John Spencer	Warren Simpson	42—31
1972	Alex Higgins	John Spencer	37—32
1973	Ray Reardon	Eddie Charlton	38—32
1974	Ray Reardon	Graham Miles	22—12
1975	Ray Reardon	Eddie Charlton	31—30
1976	Ray Reardon	Alex Higgins	27—16
1977	John Spencer	Cliff Thorburn	25—21
1978	Ray Reardon	Perrie Mans	25—18
1979	Terry Griffiths	Dennis Taylor	24—16
1980	Cliff Thorburn	Alex Higgins	18—16
1981	Steve Davis	Doug Mountjoy	18—12
1982	Alex Higgins	Ray Reardon	18—15
1983	Steve Davis	Cliff Thorburn	18— 6

Index